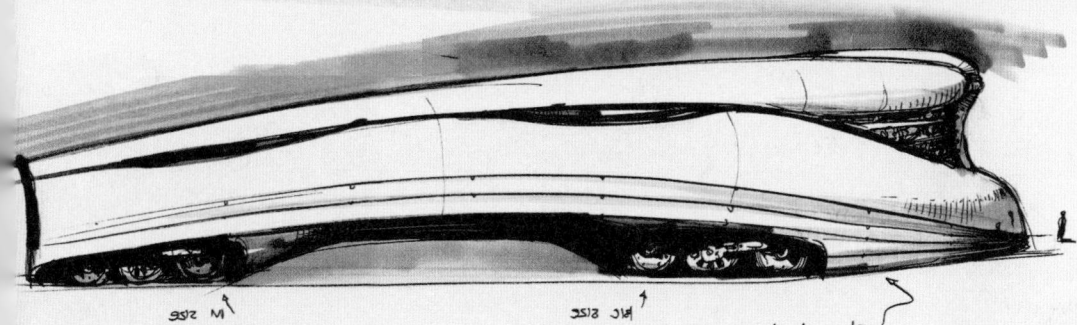

Glass stainless

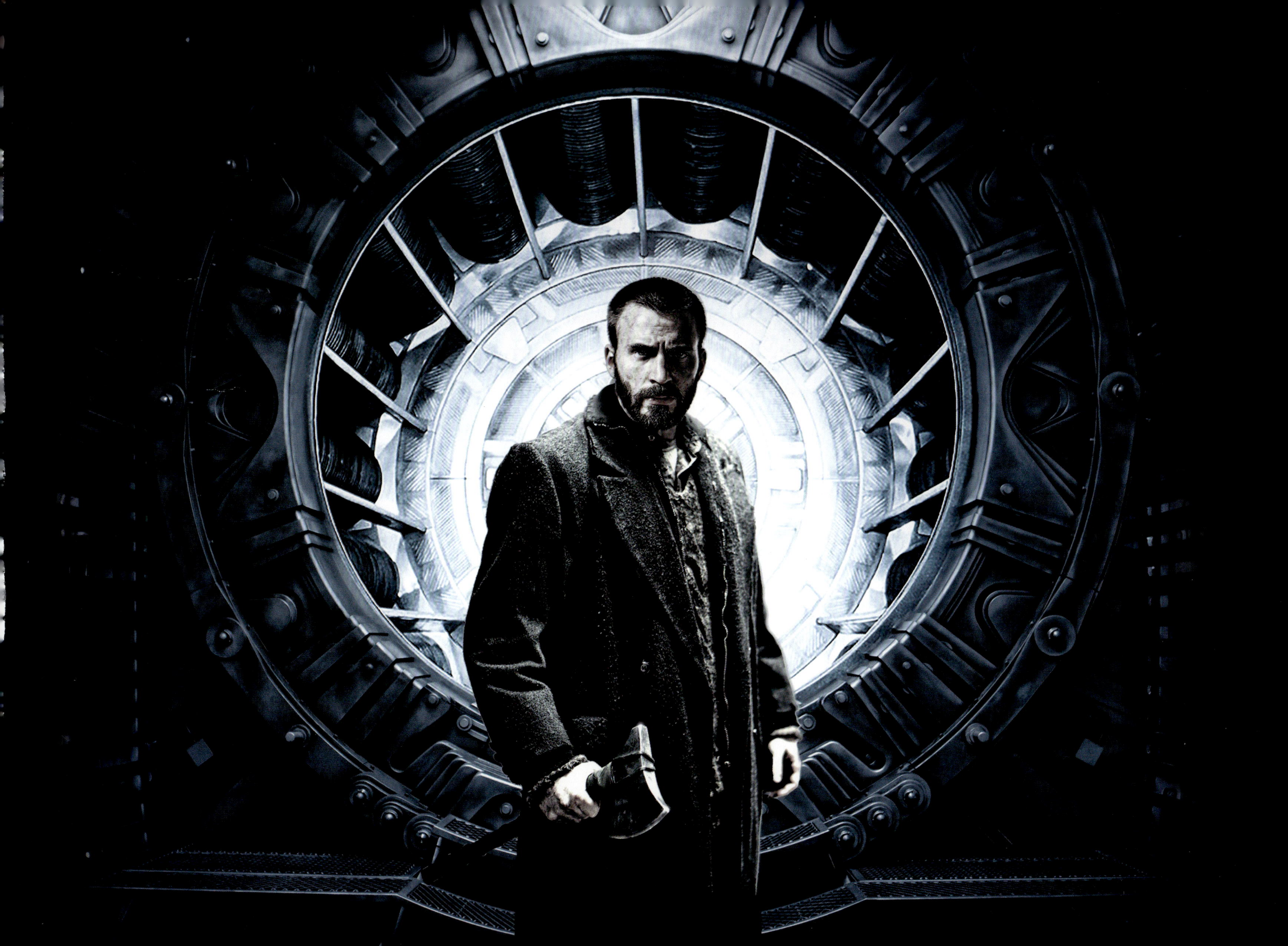

SNOWPIERCER

THE ART AND MAKING OF THE FILM

Snowpiercer: The Art and Making of the Film

Standard edition ISBN: 9781789096910
Limited edition ISBN: 9781789098235

Published by Titan Books
A division of Titan Publishing Group Ltd.
144 Southwark St.
London
SE1 0UP

First edition: August 2021

10 9 8 7 6 5 4 3 2 1

Still photography by Jae Hyuk Lee.
Concept art by Zoddd, Cho Min Soo, Jang Hee Chul, Park Jae Chul, Jakub Javora, Viktor Hoschl, and Adela Hakova.

DID YOU ENJOY THIS BOOK?
We love to hear from our readers. Please e-mail us at: readerfeedback@titanemail.com or write to Reader Feedback at the above address.
To receive advance information, news, competitions, and exclusive offers online, please sign up for the Titan newsletter on our website: www.titanbooks.com

A CIP catalogue record for this title is available from the British Library.

Printed and bound in China.

SNOWPIERCER

THE ART AND MAKING OF THE FILM

SIMON WARD

TITAN BOOKS

CONTENTS

FOREWORD

BY SCOTT FOUNDAS

One morning in July 2013, I was sitting at my desk in the New York bureau of *Variety*—where I had recently been appointed chief film critic—when the phone rang and an unexpected voice announced itself on the other end of the line. The caller was Bong Joon Ho, who I had known since his debut feature, *Barking Dogs Never Bite*, screened at the 2001 Slamdance Film Festival, but who I had neither seen nor spoken to since I'd had the pleasure of presenting his great 2009 film, *Mother*, at that year's New York Film Festival. After a few obligatory pleasantries, I detected an anxiety in Director Bong's voice, like those calls to a private detective by some wronged woman-on-the-run that kick-start the plot of many a film noir. Only here, it wasn't Bong's life that was under imminent threat, but rather that of his latest movie.

Snowpiercer represented a big gamble for Bong. After drawing Hollywood's attention with his earlier Korean films—especially 2006's boisterous creature feature, *The Host*—he had turned down all manner of American director-for-hire jobs and instead set about making his English-language debut on his own terms. Based on a French graphic novel, *Snowpiercer* would be a futuristic action-thriller, rich in Bong's signature themes of family and class struggle, set aboard a luxury passenger train circumnavigating the globe in the wake of a second ice age. The majority of the film's forty-three-million-dollar budget was supplied by leading Korean studio CJ ENM, with the US and other English-language rights having been prebought by The Weinstein Company. And that is where Bong's tale of woe began.

As we have since come to learn, a bullying, my-way-or-the-highway attitude toward filmmakers was but one—and in many respects the least—of Harvey Weinstein's manifold crimes. But in the summer of 2013, it was *Snowpiercer* that had become the latest victim of the mogul whose penchant for editing-room malfeasance had earned him the nickname 'Harvey Scissorhands.' Among other things, an exasperated Bong told me, Weinstein wanted to cut twenty minutes from *Snowpiercer*'s running time and add a voiceover narration (to be scripted by novelist Neil Gaiman). He even wanted to tack on a more definitively 'happy' ending in lieu of the open-ended (albeit hopeful) one preferred by Bong.

With the director's cut of the film about to be released in Korea and other international markets, Weinstein was holding the movie hostage in the English-speaking world, refusing to set a release date or commit to a festival premiere while he battled Bong over the cut. So Bong had hatched a plan, and this is where our phone call turned from film noir to something more like a John Le Carré espionage yarn. Being an international trade publication, *Variety* would typically review a film whenever it had its first public screening anywhere in the world (without waiting for the US release). With this in mind, Bong would dispatch Dooho Choi, the Los Angeles-based co-producer of *Snowpiercer*, to New York with a DCP [digital cinema package] of the director's cut, which he would screen for me so that I could have a review ready to run in time for the Korean opening. In an unforgettable twist, because this was a DCP of the Korean release and therefore lacking English subtitles for the Korean-language dialogue spoken by two of the film's characters, Dooho himself would sit behind me in the screening room and live-translate those scenes like the silent-film *benshi* of yore.

The rest is well-documented. My review, published on July 22, praised *Snowpiercer* as "an enormously ambitious, visually stunning and richly satisfying futuristic epic," and kicked off a tsunami of praise (from those lucky enough to see the movie) and impassioned pleas (including by Bong himself, on stage at a Museum of Modern Art tribute to *Snowpiercer* co-star, Tilda Swinton) for Weinstein to release the film in Bong's intended version. Which is eventually what happened—albeit nearly a full year later, with minimal marketing support, via Weinstein's day-and-date releasing arm, Radius. To this day, it has not had a proper cinema release in the UK. And yet, befitting a movie whose proletariat heroes trudge steadily forward despite the efforts of a megalomaniacal billionaire to silence them, *Snowpiercer* found an enthusiastic following in the US, grossing in excess of four million dollars theatrically (despite never playing wider than 350 screens) and over ten million dollars including revenue from the VOD [video on demand] launch. (It has even gone on to inspire a cable TV series.) With the triumph of *Parasite* [2019], many more are surely discovering it even as we speak—a hidden gem no more.

INTRODUCTION

"**A**cross the white immensity of an eternal winter, from one end of the frozen planet to the other, there travels a train that never stops."

So begins volume one of *Le Transperceneige*, the graphic novel originally created by Jacques Lob and Jean-Marc Rochette, published in 1982. With little to no context or warning, the first page shows a seemingly endless metallic train smashing through great drifts of snow like a bullet.

It is a bleak, formidable beginning—cold in every sense of the word. The train approaches like a warning, like the inevitability of death, and what it contains—with its passengers separated by wealth and class—is less like hope and more like kindling to ignite this tinderbox.

It was this dynamic, this powerful visual idea containing such incredible story potential, that captured the imagination of Bong Joon Ho.

The film of *Snowpiercer* is classified online as 'sci-fi,' 'action,' and 'comic book.' While those are certainly elements, it is misleading to label *Snowpiercer* so definitively. It would be like calling *The Host* (2006) a 'monster movie' or *Parasite* (2019) simply a drama. Director Bong has never been one to shy away from using genre conventions to both thrill and to smuggle in urgent messages on politics, choice, guilt, responsibility, and the environment, to name a few. His 2009 movie, *Mother,* is the most emotional movie Alfred Hitchcock never directed. With all this in mind, his adaptation of *Snowpiercer* resembles less a train and more of a Trojan Horse, hiding within its imposing façade a wealth of concerns that need discussing. Every thrilling sequence in the film has some meaning behind it—everything in the world of *Snowpiercer* is predicated on choice (on the part of the individual and society as a whole), everything has context, and everything has a cost. A rightly regarded master of playing with genre and twisting expectations, even the fundamental setup of *Snowpiercer* seems a satirical take on Hollywood blockbusters: Take the adrenalin-rush concept of a train that won't stop, but by making it a train that *never* stops, suddenly this high-concept idea becomes something more philosophical, more existential, and more interesting. More Bong Joon Ho.

The idea of the frozen world is a starting point, a catalyst to get the story going, but after that point there are no grand sci-fi ideas. It is a very grounded reality. Once we and the characters are inside the squalid conditions of the train, the narrative could just as easily be taking place one hundred years in the past as one hundred years in the future.

"The train itself has this classic and timeless feel to it," says Bong Joon Ho. "The story doesn't take place in a spaceship, and the fact that it's in a train in itself gives the story a lot of romance and this old-timey feel. This intensifies as you journey through the tail section. I really wanted the atmosphere to feel very primitive and primal—especially with the climactic fight sequence in the middle, where they fight holding onto torches. It almost feels like the people from the tail section are primitive beings and I really wanted to add that feeling to the film—the sense of being primitive, very physical, and without featuring any advanced sci-fi equipment, like laser guns. They fight with axes."

There is a relentless pace to *Snowpiercer*, a drive that carries the viewer along. The perpetual engine that moves the train and the film is our society and all the systems we have in place to continue its existence.

"The idea of the train as a free space, born out of chaos, in which these toxic 'natural orders' take root and evolve from the ground upward, is a very important one," explains actor Tilda Swinton, who plays Minister Mason. "The fantasy is one that contemplates unmediated, unchecked power-tripping: what evil mayhem might society get up to in an environment disconnected from the moral and ethical foundations that our hard-won democracies have been built on? This, of course, is a question we all currently—in 2020/21—ask ourselves daily, with a terrifying sense of urgency. In 2012, we thought we were making a dystopian parable. Little did we know."

Director Bong is asking what sort of world we have and how, on an endless loop, we can move forward. In this book, we will delve into how *Snowpiercer* was made, covering the years of hard work, examining and showcasing the behind-the-scenes process, and talking with the extraordinary individuals who helped bring this unique film to life.

ACROSS THE WHITE IMMENSITY OF AN ETERNAL WINTER, FROM ONE END OF THE FROZEN PLANET TO THE OTHER, THERE TRAVELS A TRAIN THAT NEVER STOPS.

Le Transperceneige, Jacques Lob and Jean-Marc Rochette © CASTERMAN

In 2005, Bong Joon Ho had two films to his name: *Barking Dogs Never Bite* (2000) and *Memories of Murder* (2003). *Memories of Murder* has gone on to be regarded as one of the greatest police procedural dramas ever made and was a critical and financial success. Typically, three years is about the average time Bong Joon Ho takes between movies and *The Host* would arrive in 2006, marking a major step forward in terms of logistics and scale. But before *The Host* was released on an unsuspecting public, another idea was already beginning to take root in Director Bong's mind.

An emphatic critique of society and equality, *Le Transperceneige* won the Religious Award at the 1985 Angoulême International Comics Festival. Jacques Lob and Jean-Marc Rochette would move on separately to other projects and *Snowpiercer*, despite being well regarded, was not widely known. It would, however, find its way into the hands of readers across the world over the years. Eventually, a copy landed in a comic book store near Hongik University in Seoul, where it was discovered by Bong Joon Ho.

THIS SPREAD "You couldn't put it into the 'action movie' box or comedy or sci-fi. You can't because it's something between." —Ondřej Nekvasil, production designer

OPPOSITE *Le Transperceneige*, Jacques Lob and Jean-Marc Rochette © CASTERMAN.

Le Transperceneige, Jacques Lob and Jean-Marc Rochette © CASTERMAN

Le Transperceneige, Jacques Lob and Jean-Marc Rochette © CASTERMAN

"I picked up the graphic novel in January 2005," he explains. "This was before I was in production on *The Host*. While making *The Host*, *Tokyo!* [the 2008 triptych to which Director Bong contributed a section], and *Mother*, it was almost five years that the graphic novel was in my head. While I was working on the other films, I kept thinking about this story and my thoughts were kind of all over the place. I would try this twist and that twist. It was a long process of me just experimenting with these ideas. So, when I actually turned on my laptop to begin the official writing process, I had already really let the idea mature inside and I started writing in 2010."

2005 to 2010 were somewhat of a boom time for comic book adaptations. This is before the Marvel blockbusters became all conquering and instead saw a more diverse and experimental range of comics on-screen with idiosyncratic directors behind them, including David Cronenberg's *A History of Violence* (2005), Marjane Satrapi's *Persepolis* (2007), Guillermo del Toro's more experimental sequel *Hellboy II: The Golden Army* (2008), and Edgar Wright's *Scott Pilgrim vs. the World* (2010). A lot of ink has been spilled over the faithfulness of such adaptations—and what purpose this perceived faithfulness even serves—but with *Snowpiercer*, Bong Joon Ho was not attempting to ride the cultural zeitgeist of alternative graphic novel movies. Indeed, bringing Jacques Lob and Jean-Marc Rochette's *bande dessinée* to the screen was never really his intention.

"The film is quite different from the original graphic novel in many ways," Director Bong says. "You have that basic setup of the Earth in a new ice age and humanity's last survivors on a running train with the rich people in the front cars and the poor people in the tail cars. That basic setup is still the same. That in itself is such a great premise; it was so innovative and new. But if you look into the details, pretty much everything is different, and I think during the four or five years where I let the ideas percolate, I started accumulating various ideas that weren't a part of the original graphic novel. For example, the detail where the train turns a lap every year and when they pass the bridge they all scream, 'Happy New Year!' as if the train itself is a calendar or

> ## "I THINK DURING THE FOUR OR FIVE YEARS WHERE I LET THE IDEAS PERCOLATE, I STARTED ACCUMULATING VARIOUS IDEAS THAT WEREN'T A PART OF THE ORIGINAL GRAPHIC NOVEL."
>
> BONG JOON HO

a clock. I think details like that just accumulated by themselves throughout the years."

It was only the original and initial arc of the comic book that Director Bong read and used as his jumping-off point. The later twists and turns of the subsequent volumes did not factor in. Comparing the film with the original graphic novel, there are only really two main similarities: the premise of the survivors of this new ice age living on a train divided by class, and a protagonist who is trying to make his way to the front. Proloff becomes Curtis, but Proloff is not leading a revolution like Curtis does. Much of the comic is Proloff in discussion with a female character called Belleau, as they talk about the train, the class divide, with the threat of revolution and also that the train is slowing down hanging in the background. The film foregrounds class, society, and a spirit of anger and hope in the way *Le Transperceneige* does not. There is much that is left as a mystery in the initial story arc and goes in very unexpected directions in *The Explorers*, *The Crossing*, *Terminus*, and the prequel series. *The Escape* reads like a fantastic, eerie introduction to this world; it establishes the world of *Snowpiercer* in quite an efficient way. The film builds in symbolism and themes, and creates new relationships and motifs that make it a high-concept movie, a sci-fi movie, a political movie, and a drama.

Le Transperceneige, Jacques Lob and Jean-Marc Rochette © CASTERMAN

OPPOSITE Panels from *Le Transperceneige*, originally published by Casterman in 1982.
LEFT Like the film, a great deal of action in the graphic novel is tightly framed, showing the cramped, claustrophobic conditions on board the train.
ABOVE The comic gets an on-screen cameo in the movie.

In order to help nail the dialogue and to bring out some of the themes he wanted to explore, Director Bong brought in another writer to work on his initial drafts.

"I spent 2010 adapting the graphic novel," Director Bong recalls. "Because it was my first English-language film, I had Kelly Masterson help me as the co-writer. I discovered him from the very last feature film of Sidney Lumet, *Before the Devil Knows You're Dead* [2007]. It features Philip Seymour Hoffman and Ethan Hawke, and it's a very powerful family story about a father and son, but at the same time it's also a crime drama, and that left a huge impression on me. I really appreciated the fact that on the credits it only had one person as the writer. Usually, if you have

three or four screenwriters, you don't know who wrote which part, so I was really sure that I wanted to work with this person. With *Snowpiercer,* you can also think about the film as the father-and-son archetype: you have Gilliam and Curtis, and Wilford and Curtis, who sort of form this father-and-son-like relationship, and I think that's why I was particularly drawn to Kelly Masterson.

"Kelly wrote a lot of stage plays before transitioning into film, so he has a way of creating dialogue that's very concise and powerful but illustrates the depth of the characters. In terms of the overall structure of the film, the basic sci-fi ideas, and the visual descriptions, a lot of those came from me, but with the dialogue, I really received a lot of help from Kelly."

"[DIRECTOR BONG]'S A GENUINELY INTERESTED AND CURIOUS MAN, AND I THINK HIS FILMS, ALTHOUGH THEY ARE ALL ENTERTAINING AND WITTY, THEY ALL HAVE A STREAK OF MISCHIEF IN THEM, AND FUN. HE REALLY ENGAGES WITH THE HUMAN CONDITION, THE PROBLEMS OF THE HUMAN CONDITION, AND HUMAN SOCIETY."

EWEN BREMNER

"THE MOST NOTICEABLE DIFFERENCE WAS TILDA'S GREAT SPEECH AS MINISTER MASON, AND THIS IS WHEN KELLY MASTERSON JOINED IN THE PROCESS AND CONTRIBUTED HIS WRITING TO THE SCRIPT."

BONG JOON HO

"There were many drafts where small details changed," explains Bong Joon Ho. "But I think there were three drafts that had major shifts in the storyline. One of the things that my first draft didn't contain was the whole scene where Curtis and Namgoong sit across from each other before they enter the engine car and tell these confession stories from times past. This is when Curtis confesses that he once ate a baby, and a lot of people in the tail section cut off their arms for other people to eat. That whole shocking scene was not a part of my first draft. In that draft, just before they enter the engine car, Namgoong is talking about this not being a wall but a door and we must break the door and go outside, and that kronole is actually a huge bomb. I added that whole confession scene in the second draft, and that really brought a major shift in the story. That was a major shift that happened from the first step to the second step. I think it would be wrong to call these 'drafts'—there were a lot of drafts in between but there were three major steps."

One of the defining moments of the film came from Kelly, brought to such vivid life on the screen by Tilda Swinton. This was part of the drafting and revision process where, like in a revolution, tiny incremental changes eventually lead to bigger milestones.

"From the second step to the third step, the most noticeable difference was Tilda's great speech as Minister Mason, and this is when Kelly Masterson joined in the process and contributed his writing to the script. That whole section where Minister Mason puts a shoe on top of Ewen's character, makes this analogy about a shoe, and she says, 'be a shoe'—that was written by Kelly Masterson. He wrote that amazing speech and that was one of the major differences from step two to step three."

Bong Joon Ho spends years planning his next project and *Snowpiercer* was no different. However, the screenplay was only one part of his meticulous preparations. While getting the story where it needed to be on the page, in parallel, he began to look at artwork to visualize just how his Snowpiercer would look on the screen.

THIS SPREAD "It's kind of a scary thought but the world has become more like the world in this movie." —Dooho Choi

CHAPTER TWO

CASTING THE FILM

Snowpiercer is Bong Joon Ho's first film not entirely in Korean, but that does not make it automatically an English-language movie populated by only American actors. Far from it. Korean is still spoken throughout and the cast is unusually diverse for what can be labeled as a 'high-concept film.' The characters populating the train are from different backgrounds, with different attitudes, looks, and wants, and they are played by a mixture of recognizable faces, international stars, character actors, and living legends.

RIGHT All of the drawings done throughout the film were drawn by original *Le Transperceneige* artist Jean-Marc Rochette. "When we see the painter's hand sketching [in the film], it is Rochette's hand." —Dooho Choi

> ## "[SONG KANG HO AND KO ASUNG] WERE PRETTY MUCH ON BOARD *SNOWPIERCER* SINCE 2009 WHEN I TALKED WITH THEM ABOUT BEING A PART OF THIS PROJECT."
>
> BONG JOON HO

"Song Kang Ho and Ko Asung played the father and daughter in *The Host* (2006)," explains Bong Joon Ho. "They were pretty much on board *Snowpiercer* since 2009 when I talked with them about being a part of this project. They're actors that I love very much, but that wasn't really all of it. I knew that the story in itself—the basic setting, where you have survivors on a train—would require a diverse cast from diverse nations and various races and various skin tones. I knew from the very beginning when I started adapting the graphic novel that in the ten or so main characters there would naturally be some Korean actors."

Producer Dooho Choi echoes this thought process, "He wrote the screenplay with Song Kang Ho and Ko Asung in mind. In terms of everyone else, Tilda Swinton and John Hurt were the first English-speaking actors who were asked. They were fans of Director Bong's previous films and it was a pretty smooth process getting them on board. Once we attached John and Tilda, other actors became excited about working on the project.

"I think at the time there were people who were familiar with Director Bong's films, and there were just as many people who weren't familiar with his films. I'm sure some of the people we ended up working with became familiar with his filmography only afterward. But John and Tilda knew his films and were big fans, and that really got things going."

This is certainly true of several actors who worked on *Snowpiercer*—even though *The Host* had received a great deal of acclaim and was a massive box-office success in South Korea, they weren't wholly familiar with Bong Joon Ho's filmography. The New Korean Cinema wave had not yet peaked and, arguably, is only really now understood and defined in retrospect.

Ed Harris confirms that when he was first offered a role in *Snowpiercer*, he had some catching up to do. "When I was asked to do this movie, didn't know about Director Bong's work. I went and watched some of his movies—*The Host*, *Mother* [2009], *Memories of Murder* [2003]—and thought, *Wow, I've got to work with this guy*. I really enjoyed it. I liked Director Bong very much. I liked working with him a lot... I just like working, period, especially when you've seen someone's work and you have that much faith in their vision. You're really just trying to fulfil their vision, and so you have a lot of confidence in the director. You're in good hands. You trust them implicitly."

A sentiment echoed by Jamie Bell: "I was swayed by him as a filmmaker, and after that, I went back and looked at his other works. I think I'd seen *The Host* before, but I'd never put that together—that it was him. I think that was a lot of people's first introduction to him. I then went back and watched *Mother*, and *Memories of Murder*, and then I felt stupid because I didn't realize that what was before me was the opportunity to work with an auteur filmmaker."

Much of the cast shared similar experiences about how they came aboard the film. Typically, once the formal approaches had been made, they sat down with Bong and he explained the movie by letting his artwork tell the story. Ewen Bremner relates, "I watched a bunch of his films and went down to meet him. He and Dooho explained the film to me and he showed me a lot of the artwork that he was working from. He's a completely visual filmmaker, so orientated by visual storytelling."

THIS SPREAD The cast and crew on set.

"I HAVE A LOT OF GREAT MEMORIES ABOUT JOHN.
HE WAS ACTUALLY THE FIRST ACTOR TO 'BOARD
THE TRAIN' DURING THE CASTING PROCESS."

BONG JOON HO

The first actor to officially sign onto the film was Sir John Hurt. Having such an iconic actor involved was not only an incredible cou[...] but also gave the filmmakers a boost of confidence.

"I have a lot of great memories about John," says Bong Joon Ho. "He was actually the first actor to 'board the train' during the castin[g] process. But before he even joined the cast, when Dooho and I me[t] him in London, he was very encouraging. From his perspective, we must have seemed like indie filmmakers from Asia and at that poin[t] we weren't even able to give him the script—we could only sho[w] him a couple of conceptual artwork pieces. But after seeing those he said that he thought this sci-fi film would turn out great and h[e] provided so much encouragement and support. It really felt lik[e] he was part of the team from the very beginning."

THIS SPREAD "The fun of the film from a makeup point of view was that all the characters needed 'character' makeup. Each had their own distinctive look, varying from full-body tattoos for Luke Pasqualino's character, Grey, to John Hurt's home-cut hairdo and sores. So all the characters required some considerable work to make them fit into their environments. The fron[t] of the train had a gloss and clean precision, while the back of the train was grubby, badly kept, and bedraggled." —Jeremy Woodhead, hair and makeup designer

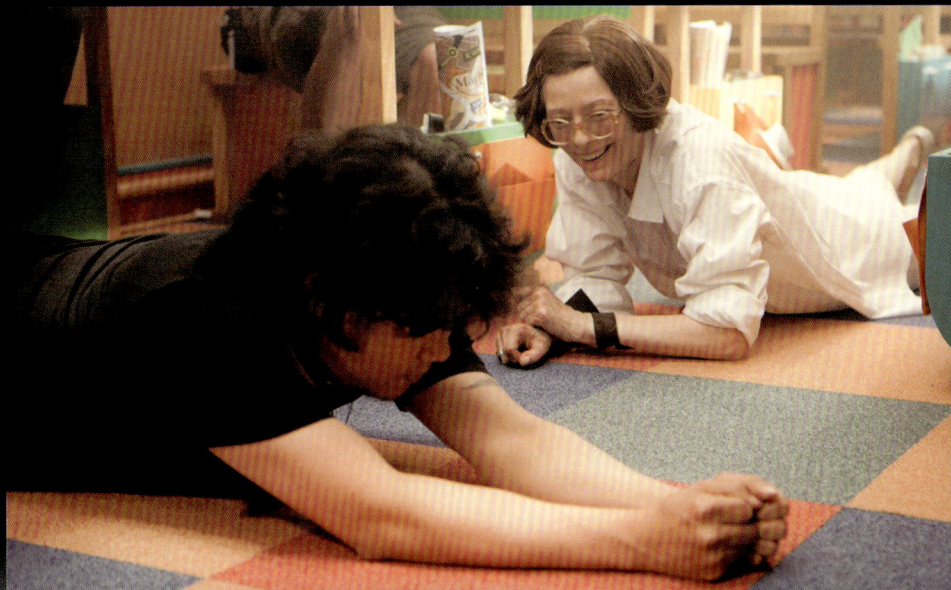

Another actor who became 'part of the team' and has continued to be ever since is Tilda Swinton. An acclaimed, Academy Award®-winning performer, Swinton was well aware of Bong Joon Ho before working with him. As most enduring friendships start, their initial conversation wasn't so much a matter of discussing work and business but more a general meeting of minds.

"When we met in Cannes for the first time, over a great big breakfast in my hotel room, we knew pretty much within the first croissant that we were going to be friends and probably collaborators," remembers Swinton. "He mentioned right then and there that he was in the throes of plans for *Snowpiercer* and how, as it happened, there was no role for me in it. We simply shrugged and said, 'Next time, soon, yes please,' and continued to tuck in. What he described to me was certainly intriguing: as I remember, he told it to me as a kind of political thriller, dystopian escape movie. After *Mother*, this sounded like an exhilarating turn in the road."

The key role, the main character we are following throughout and who would end up being front and center of all the eventual marketing and promotional material, was Curtis. This determined fighter but reluctant leader was played on-screen by Chris Evans. Evans had already worked with some distinctive voices such as Edgar Wright and Danny Boyle, and he was well aware of Bong Joon Ho before *Snowpiercer* came onto his radar.

"I had seen Bong's other work," he confirms. "I knew he was an incredible filmmaker, an incredible artist, an incredible voice. To be honest, his confidence, his stillness as a person, is what kind of bred such allegiance in me. I had a few questions, but it wasn't necessarily like my questions were given answers, it's more that I just became captivated by Bong. There was just something about him that I was excited about. Something about him that just told me: *hitch your wagon to this guy, he knows what he's doing and he's going to make something special.*"

Having a cast that represented a microcosm of society was essential to Director Bong but proved a challenge. As Dooho Choi explains, the matter of getting this international team to an Eastern European set was a major undertaking. "For me, the logistical challenge was coordinating with the art department and talent reps to ensure the actors would be in Prague when the sets they'd be working on were ready. We couldn't afford to build all the sets at once and keep them up. Throughout the shoot, the art department was building and tearing down sets, and building new ones, so it was a unique situation managing the construction schedule and talent availability."

"I HAD SEEN BONG'S OTHER WORK. I KNEW HE WAS AN INCREDIBLE FILMMAKER, AN INCREDIBLE ARTIST, AN INCREDIBLE VOICE. TO BE HONEST, HIS CONFIDENCE, HIS STILLNESS AS A PERSON, IS WHAT KIND OF BRED SUCH ALLEGIANCE IN ME."

CHRIS EVANS

But once everyone was ready to get to work, there quickly emerged a sense of harmony and togetherness, not unlike the sense of comradeship among the rebels in the film itself.

"I'd met Chris Evans before and Tilda is represented by my agent, so we had a little bit of a connection there," says Bell. "We'd worked with similar directors. Tilda had worked with David Mackenzie, so I'd heard a lot about Tilda from him. It felt a bit like a family in a way... [During the] making of it, Bong was very free with us. I think he was that way with all the actors. He was very willing to give us the playing field. That's a sign to me of a good director—he trusted his actors and his actors trust him, then there's this relationship that you have and people are willing to go further and do more for you."

THIS SPREAD "The actors were very involved in their looks, of course, but we had to steer a course where all the various inhabitants of the train could be located by their look—the rear grubby and malnourished, with worn in dirt and subtle sores on their skin that suggested underlying illness and poor diet. So the film had to have a 'family' of characters at the rear—all equally dirty, and unkempt. The front passengers gave us much more freedom to show the eccentricity of the story. Claude had her dolly hair do and the teacher (Alison Pill) was almost a throwback to the American mom of the '50s." —Jeremy Woodhead

CURTIS

For Chris Evans, *Snowpiercer* came along at exactly the right moment in his career. After more than a decade of indie movies, eye-catching supporting roles, and eventual leads in major tentpole pictures, playing the protagonist in what is essentially an English-language Korean production was the challenge he was looking for.

"I had made a decision in my mind around that time that I was done working with directors that were question marks," Evans explains. "You can have an unbelievable script, you can have an unbelievable role, you can have an unbelievable cast or producers or a giant budget, but unless you have a quality storyteller, you really have nothing. I think we've all seen films where on paper it checks a lot of boxes but for some reason it doesn't come together. Even the inverse of that where maybe the script isn't fully there and you don't have the budget and the cast is full of unknowns, but the director knew what they were doing, and as a result the project sings. I had kind of just chosen: work with storytellers. I had seen Bong's other films and each one was just so specific and so beautiful and poetic. Every single project had such a specific flavor and I was just excited to go to work with him."

The character of Curtis is not a hero. The audience may be rooting for him to make it to the front of the train, but this is not a movie about good versus evil. Curtis is a human, one with darkness in his past. There is something about the look of the tail-section passengers and the treatment of them that brings to mind prisoners of war. They are the last humans and Evans saw in Curtis an opportunity to discuss survivor's guilt.

"YOU CAN HAVE AN UNBELIEVABLE SCRIPT, YOU CAN HAVE AN UNBELIEVABLE ROLE, YOU CAN HAVE AN UNBELIEVABLE CAST OR PRODUCERS OR A GIANT BUDGET, BUT UNLESS YOU HAVE A QUALITY STORYTELLER, YOU REALLY HAVE NOTHING."

CHRIS EVANS

OPPOSITE Curtis poses with his weapon of choice, which will soon be blood-soaked. **LEFT** Evans and Director Bong on set during a break in filming.

"CURTIS WAS PART OF A SITUATION WHERE IT WAS LIFE OR DEATH, AND HE WENT DOWN A DARK PATH AND THEN HAS TO LIVE WITH THAT SHAME."

CHRIS EVANS

"I think it's a real examination of guilt and shame, the capacity of our own depths—what we're capable of when pushed. Curtis was part of a situation where it was life or death, and he went down a dark path and then has to live with that shame. The funny thing about shame is that no matter how much you examine it, no matter how much you confront it, it never goes away. You just find a way to cope, but the echo of that guilt will always resonate and it can either tear you down or it can propel you to try to be better. I think Curtis is this walking embodiment of that shame and that guilt and that self-loathing, but it's a catalyst for him to try to fight for other people and fight to reclaim some humanity, to reclaim some of his honor that he felt he'd lost," says Evans.

Things get worse for Curtis before they get better. There is bloodshed and more guilt, and getting to the front of the train becomes a purely physical compulsion. The real drama is the decisions he is faced with along the way and if he can make the selfless choice. By finally liberating the train, he can liberate himself from his past.

BELOW Curtis interrogates Minister Mason.
BELOW RIGHT Curtis makes it to Wilford's domain, flanked by Claude.

It is a relentless journey for Curtis and the demands placed upon Evans were substantial. "Chris was 100% committed from day one," says Dooho Choi. "I think it's one of his best performances. Although he's known for playing Captain America and has that all-American hero quality, he had also made a series of smaller independent films where he played more conflicted characters. When Director Bong saw *Puncture* (2011), he knew Chris was right for the part. And the role required a lot of action, so we were fortunate to have someone who'd had so much experience with stunts. He did all the action so gracefully, no matter how physically demanding the sequence. Never got injured, completely safe."

Bong Joon Ho agrees, "At this point, he had already shot one of the *Captain America* movies, and the stunt coordinator commented on how Chris Evans is just like a stunt machine. He leaves no room for error and has impeccable timing. He was just perfect in terms of his stunt sequences, didn't need to rehearse, so actually a lot of the stunt men were pretty nervous about making mistakes with him."

This is confirmed by Julian Spencer, the stunt coordinator, who worked closely with Evans on the movie's key fight sequence. "With Chris it was a matter of just throwing him in. Between takes he'd still come up to me and get frustrated because he was used to having all this choreographed, and I said, 'No, don't worry, it's fucking amazing.' You can see him physically looking around then suddenly jumping because something else has come from that way. It's all real."

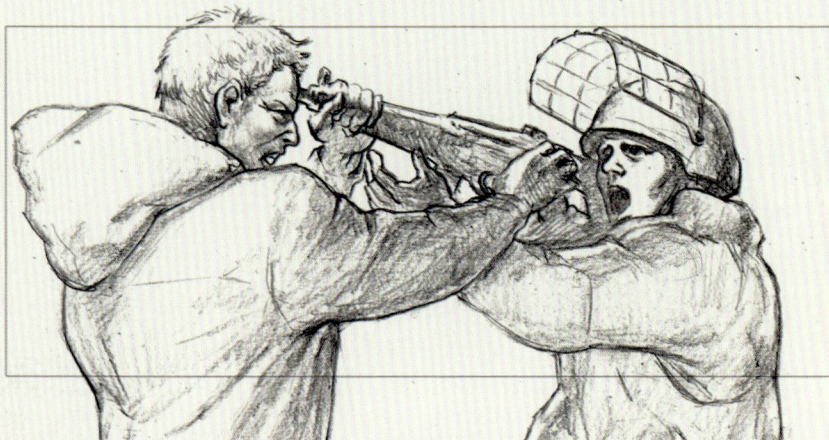

THIS PAGE "On Curtis's coat there's some very specific detail. On his shoulder there's a tape detail, like some sort of insulation tape, and then stitched on top." —Catherine George, costume designer

OPPOSITE PAGE Original and final design for Curtis, compared with *Le Transperceneige*'s male protagonist, Proloff. "We had four or five possibilities for his coat, and the one I thought was going to work was a sort of green fatigue color, but looking at the fitting photographs, you really see that at some point, he put on this charcoal-grey, almost black coat that's sort of longer, almost over-sized, and it just made the character come to life again." —Catherine George

Le Transperceneige, Jacques Lob and Jean-Marc Rochette © CASTERMAN

> "WE HAD FOUR OR FIVE POSSIBILITIES FOR HIS COAT, AND THE ONE I THOUGHT WAS GOING TO WORK WAS A SORT OF GREEN FATIGUE COLOR, BUT LOOKING AT THE FITTING PHOTOGRAPHS, YOU REALLY SEE THAT AT SOME POINT, HE PUT ON THIS CHARCOAL-GREY, ALMOST BLACK COAT THAT'S SORT OF LONGER, ALMOST OVER-SIZED, AND IT JUST MADE THE CHARACTER COME TO LIFE AGAIN."
>
> CATHERINE GEORGE

What also helped to make it all feel real was the incredible attention paid to makeup and costuming, creating layers and layers of detail that may not be noticed by the audience on a surface level but all contribute toward the feeling of desperation, neglect, and the harshness of life in the tail section.

"We tried a few wigs on Chris during earlier tests to suggest a time lapse and to take him away from the clean-cut look," explains hair and makeup designer Jeremy Woodhead. "We ended up going the other way and making it shorter and clipped closer to his head. This was a much stronger look and allowed for the strength of his face to come through. His character was multi-layered and it was important that the subtleties of his performance were not compromised by too much hair! Enough to make him grungy, and have his skin look unhealthy with sores and blotches. A [long] way away from Captain America!"

"It was about hiding some of his muscles," says costume designer Catherine George. "They all wear so many layers. If you have possessions, you need to wear them all at once. We did a lot of research into people in homeless situations and refugee camps, so Curtis had a lot of layers on. I think he has a thermal shirt, a sweater, and a coat, but we had to cut it all away. We had a couple of versions with sleeves in case he took his coat off, and we had versions where the sleeves were cut away under the overcoat so it could look a little more droopy on him and cover up his physique. The hat kind of made a difference, too. I thought it was altogether like something we had never seen Chris Evans in before. It really made him look different and changed his regular 'hero' look."

This approach works not only for the viewers but for Evans, too, helping him discover this non-hero who finds himself leading a revolution. "Incredibly helpful. More so than even some of the other films I've done where clearly a costume goes a long way in terms of bringing the character to life. But this film in particular, just because it tells the history. It's not just a matter of who I am today based on these clothes, it's who I've been for these past few years and it just shows the struggle."

MINISTER MASON

Minister Mason, as depicted by Tilda Swinton, is one of the most memorable, fascinating, and impactful characters to come from a film so far this century. The detail of the costuming and makeup, through to the physicality and voice, all combines to make Mason a creation unlike any other. There is almost something of the train wreck about Mason—you can't not look at her/him.

"My portrait of the despotic self-aggrandizing, ludicrously posturing semi-clown was drawn from a wide range of lethally dangerous buffoons—from Hitler and Mussolini, via Gaddafi, Thatcher, and Idi Amin to the Kims of North Korea and Silvio Berlusconi—but the nightmare of recent casting across the globe is beyond everything we imagined. I was—with a now-poignant lack of awareness of incarnations yet to come—particularly interested in how often society harbors, and even advances, outsize and even ridiculous and somewhat infantilized leaders... As if a certain protective fondness grows up around them and a taste for the distractions provided by the drama—and comedy—they provide are key to their success, even in democratic elections... The now-familiar instance [being] the antic pantomime mummer, with grotesquely exaggerated gestures, bizarre and somehow compassion-inducing details of appearance (mad makeup and bonkers hair—an essential 'tell')... In any case, the concept of Mason as somehow self-elected and self-entitled is key. The wig, the teeth, the meaningless handmade medals and uniforms, and the crucial deep well of cowardice and self-interest.

"He/she is a poltroon who has made a deal with the devil of self-interest above all. Therefore, is beyond help or hope."

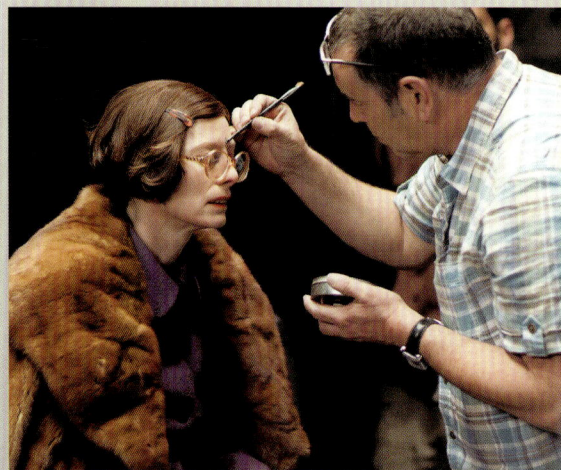

THIS SPREAD "I loved to think about Mason's cabin. A teddy on the lower bunk... a kettle and a supply of Tetley's tea bags and jammy dodger biscuits... a crossword book lying on top of some fascist tome... About the block he/she rested the wig on, about a mirror surrounded by bare light bulbs like that of a Broadway chorus girl... About the way in which stepping out into the rest of the train meant 'SHOWTIME!'" —Tilda Swinton

"THE ACCENT WAS BASED ON MY OLD NANNY. MASON'S IS HER VOICE. IT WAS A SPECIAL PRESENT TO MY BROTHERS."

TILDA SWINTON

"WE WERE DOING HER UNIFORM AND ORIGINALLY WE THOUGHT IT WAS GOING TO BE DARK NAVY. THEN WE SAW THE GADDAFI PICTURE WITH HIS WHITE UNIFORM. ALSO, WE REALIZED THAT ON THE TRAIN, FOR THE SCENE WITH THE AXE SOLDIERS, THAT IT WOULD BE MUCH MORE IMPACTFUL IF SHE WAS IN WHITE."

CATHERINE GEORGE

Tilda Swinton expresses that she is undecided on Mason's gender and, indeed, the final shooting script refers to Mason as 'he.' Before the famous 'Be a Shoe' speech, when Fuyu (Stephen Park) hands the microphone to Mason, he says, "Seven minutes allotted for your speech, sir." Throughout the entire scriptwriting process, Mason was written as a man.

"Mason, in the first place, is not actually anything other than a construct," says Swinton. "He/she is a complete fake." So just as Mason, as a passenger on the train, is created from the elements he/she pieces together to form an identity, so the role for Swinton came together by experimenting with the look and the accessories—finding all the parts that would make 'the Mason suit.'"

OPPOSITE Minister Mason watches the axe fight, flanked by Fuyu (played by Stephen Park) and the Franco brothers (played by Vlad Ivanov and Adnan Hasković).
RIGHT Minister Mason gets to sample what passes for nutrition in the tail section: the notorious protein blocks.
BELOW Early concept art showing Minister Mason in the original, male iteration.

Costume designer Catherine George, who had worked with Swinton on 2011's *We Need to Talk About Kevin*, recalls unearthing Mason as a collaboration between her, Tilda, Director Bong, and Dooho Choi. "We all went to Tilda's house, which was a blast. It's a very strong memory of going to her house, eating fish pies, and the dogs were jumping around, and having this suitcase full of clothes. We were just basically dressing up and drinking wine. We'd play with glasses and teeth, and all kinds of stuff. It's really kind of delightful, that moment when actors try something on and suddenly it's 'Oh, there she is!'"

"I do remember," says Swinton, "that I put a pie in the oven and told everybody that we had about twenty minutes before it would be ready, and somehow, we reached that enduring shape and concept before we sat down to eat."

For any perfectly costumed character, their look works not only visually on-screen but also for how it informs and explains the character. In the case of Mason, every detail tells a story. "For Mason's military look, we talked a lot about leaders," explains Catherine George. "At one point, we found this picture of Gaddafi where he's getting off a plane in Italy and he's made his own medal patch. It was like barcodes. Those things really tickle people, and Mason's doing this. She's mainly made those medals from stuff she's found on the train, so that's basically what we did."

When the first promotional photos from Snowpiercer began to appear in 2013, many articles referred to Swinton as 'unrecognizable' as Mason and a huge part of that is the makeup. Again, aside from the impact Mason makes when he/she appears on the screen before the filthy and malnourished tail sectioners, every part of Mason is a glimpse into this power-hungry and highly insecure bureaucrat's psychology.

THIS SPREAD "The wig was like a rather scratchy woollen hat... The lipstick was essential, the final touch as she strapped on her removable breasts and puffed up her chest."—Tilda Swinton
ABOVE Tilda Swinton trying on costumes in her home.

"THE TEETH WERE LIKE THAT THING YOU DO AS CHILDREN, OF STUFFING ORANGE PEEL GNASHERS IN YOUR MOUTH AT HALLOWEEN WHEN DRESSING UP AS A WITCH."

TILDA SWINTON

ABOVE Division of Birds, National Museum of Natural History, Smithsonian Institution. Photo by Chip Clark. "This image was so important for Mason's look." —Catherine George
RIGHT Costume designs by Catherine George. "She's this middling bureaucrat who's got visions of grandeur." —Catherine George

"Working with Tilda is always a treat—rare amongst actors," explains hair and makeup designer Jeremy Woodhead. "She has no vanity and is eager to explore 'character' from the get-go. We tried several wigs, but she loved that look we ended up with, which was a really nasty cheap store-bought wig, that suggested that Mason was in fact bald underneath—or was she?

"I gave Tilda a false nose, designed to hide a bit of engineering that pulled her own nose up to make it more piggy. To emphasise this and to change the balance of Tilda's face, we gave her prominent shorter teeth with more gum on show. This changed the shape of Tilda's mouth and I think helped her embrace the accent of Mason.

"Tilda's 'beauty' makeup was designed to suggest that her need for glasses compromised her close vision, too—her lipstick was applied without care and the eyebrows pencilled in with no clear vision."

The final flourish was an accidental discovery. Production designer Ondřej Nekvasil was showing Bong Joon Ho a photo he had found that he felt could be useful for one of the set designs. The photo showed a long, thin room with dozens of drawers opened outward to display hundreds of dead birds. In the middle of the Smithsonian Museum's colorful collection stands scientist Roxie Laybourne. With her large glasses, purple suit, and neatly combed, precisely clipped hair, she reminded Director Bong of someone.

"Bong saw it and said, 'Look at this amazing picture,'" recalls Catherine George. "I said, 'It looks like some of the research I've done for Mason,' so it just kind of came together."

EDGAR

Edgar is Curtis's second-in-command during the rebellion. He was born on the train and has lived all his life in the tail section. He is full of energy, hope, and determination—he is everything that Curtis seems to be fighting for; something Curtis runs the risk of forgetting.

Edgar is portrayed on-screen by Jamie Bell, the British star of *Billy Elliot* (2000), *The Adventures of Tintin* (2011), *Rocketman* (2019), and many others. What he responded to in *Snowpiercer* was its alternative nature to other films and Bong Joon Ho's take on the material. "I couldn't really place what the film was, couldn't place if it was a piece of science fiction. Conventionally, it doesn't feel like part of the Hollywood system in any way. It's clearly speaking to much bigger themes: geo-political themes, inequality, themes of revolution. These are things that are very up front and very foreground in the movie, and usually—in Hollywood systems, in the action films—maybe they'll start hinting at that stuff but it would be very background, very subtext if at all.

"So I had no idea what this was, what it was supposed to feel like, where it was supposed to sit in the market, and that was exciting. Something felt so 'rogue' about this movie from the outset—what it was trying to do, what it was trying to say. Obviously, I then went and met with Director Bong... As soon as I met him, I felt the creative energy that he has. It's kind of effervescent, it comes from him, it can't help but escape him in the way that he would describe what it meant. 'The whole world's on this train, everything that we understand is on this train, everything that we have to fight for is on this train.' I was just really inspired by him and his passion for it."

OPPOSITE TOP RIGHT Beside the Painter, Edgar looks at the outside world—an unknown place.
OPPOSITE BELOW RIGHT Jamie Bell, Bong Joon Ho, Dooho Choi, and the Czech stuntmen prepare for Edgar's climactic scene. "The Czech stunt guys are phenomenally brutal and great performers. They really go for it and give their all."—Julian Spencer

"I HAD NO IDEA WHAT THIS WAS,
WHAT IT WAS SUPPOSED TO FEEL LIKE,
WHERE IT WAS SUPPOSED TO SIT IN
THE MARKET, AND THAT WAS EXCITING.
SOMETHING FELT SO 'ROGUE' ABOUT
THIS MOVIE FROM THE OUTSET."

JAMIE BELL

The overarching story of *Snowpiercer* is Curtis's very literal journey, but the beating heart of the film is Edgar, one of the few unequivocally likeable characters in the film. In this dire situation, the viewer has in Edgar someone to root for and empathise with. He is, in other words, innocent. Bell brought his own experiences and history to bear in his performance.

"He is an interesting character," says Bell. "He doesn't know any different. He has a kind of uneducated curiosity about him because he has no other perspective; all he has is the interior of this train. He's infantilized... He's the one who's been told exactly what to do, what to eat, and all his understanding of the outside world has come through narratives, not through experience. Obviously, within the character is a burning sense of *I want it to change* as well as *I want to experience these things first hand, I want to know what this was like for everybody else*. I admire those kinds of characters. I feel it as a working-class kid growing up in a place that did feel forgotten, that did feel oppressed, living in the North East of England. Especially when one of the central characters of this is based directly on Thatcher, someone who's directly responsible for ruining parts of my community—it felt very personal, and I found that personal element within it. I never talked to Bong specifically about that. I was obviously unaware of what Tilda was doing until we got to the set. This was never talked about, but it sat personally with me"

OPPOSITE BOTTOM LEFT The makeup department touches up Bell's wounds in between shots.
OPPOSITE BOTTOM RIGHT "What [Director Bong] was trying to achieve was some moments of genuine fear from you when you didn't know what was coming at you, you didn't know to react because no one's told you how to react." —Jamie Bell

"WE CAME UP WITH THIS OVERSIZED BOILER SUIT, WHICH REALLY DID MAKE ME FEEL LIKE A BIT OF A KID, ALMOST LIKE WEARING DAD'S CLOTHES, AND THAT WAS AN IDEA FROM CATHERINE OR BONG. IT SPOKE TO HOW MUCH THIS CHARACTER DOESN'T KNOW: THERE'S SO MUCH ABOUT THE WORLD HE'S UNAWARE OF. EDGAR IS QUITE PLAYFUL. HE'S FOUND HIS PLAYGROUND IN A WAY; HE'S TURNED THIS HIDEOUSNESS INTO HIS OWN PLAYGROUND."

JAMIE BELL

While the visual creation of Minister Mason was key, costuming and makeup were just as important to each and every character, including Edgar, as Bell explains: "Bong was like, 'No-one's going to look pretty in this, you can't look pretty when you're living in a slum.' With all that dirt and filth every day, it would be impossible. For a lot of us actors, it was quite unsettling: 'What do you mean? Obviously, we're going to look pretty, aren't we? Don't you want us to look like we're white-toothed and handsome?!' And he said no, I want you to look like you've got bad acne, I want you to have skin rashes, diseases. Edgar has them on his face if you look really closely. We had prosthetics put in specific places: skin lesions, bumps, rashes, grime, and filth. And that played also into the clothes we were wearing as well. For me and Catherine George, what we really wanted to do was enhance the idea that you don't have any of your own clothes; all your clothes are handed down to you. These are all clothes that came from people who had passed away or from other people on the train who have died or whatever. We wanted to maintain that sense that he's the child pretending to be a man, pretending to be a revolutionary."

GILLIAM

"Gilliam (70s), sits against the back wall of the train, wrapped entirely in rag-like clothes with only his face protruding."

This is how Gilliam is described in the screenplay. When he moves through the crowd, he is treated with reverence and respect. Few actors naturally carry the type of respect that comes from thoughtfulness and calm intelligence, but then there were very few actors like Sir John Hurt.

In a legendary career that spanned everything from *Alien* (1979) to *Only Lovers Left Alive* (2013), via *Midnight Express* (1978) and *The Elephant Man* (1980), Hurt received no shortage of accolades for his performances. But it was his inquisitiveness and love of acting that kept him working up until his death in 2017.

ABOVE Concept art of Gilliam sans the left-hand wooden handle replacement.
RIGHT "When John passed away, I was so grateful that I'd had those few weeks with him. Everyone was moved and touched by him. He was a real pro, he really was." —Jamie Bell

"JOHN HURT WAS VERY OPTIMISTIC ABOUT THE PROJECT AND REALLY GAVE US A LOT OF SUPPORT."

BONG JOON HO

The character of Gilliam is a 'wise man' and the spiritual leader of the tail section. Everyone looks to him for guidance, even though his genuine care and affection for his fellow survivors is eventually undercut by the revelation that he was working with Wilford to maintain the balance and 'harmony' of the train. It is a role unlike any he had taken on before, for a director unlike any he had worked with before, and getting him on board the project proved less challenging than one would assume for an actor of his standing.

"We met John at the Soho Hotel in London," co-producer Dooho Choi reminisces. "What can I tell you about that meeting? It was a very lively meeting! Director Bong had a lot to say about John's work in *Alien* and also *The Elephant Man*, and it was decided right then and there. He was excited that he would be in the film and I remember John giving Bong a big bear hug at the end of the meeting. He said, 'I'm doing it!' and that was that."

"JOHN HURT IS AN ACTOR WHO REPRESENTS FILM HISTORY—
HE'S A BREATHING PART OF IT AND AS A FILM BUFF MYSELF,
I REMEMBER SHARING SO MANY FUN CONVERSATIONS IN
BETWEEN SHOOTS, JUST OVER A CUP OF COFFEE."

BONG JOON HO

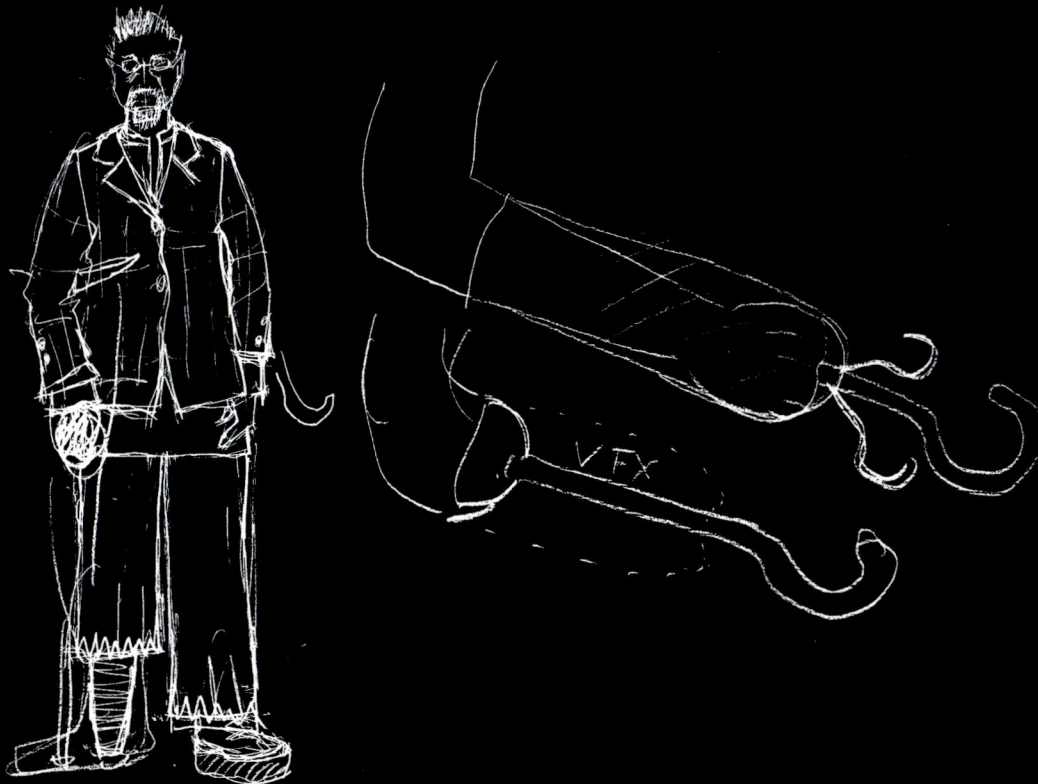

The role required that he dressed in rags, be covered in dirt, and get around with a missing arm and leg. So that was what Hurt did. And while they discussed the best way to hide his leg using a green sock that could be digitally removed in postproduction, it was decided that primarily practical effects would work best. Catherine George explains, "His leg was tied back. I think we had talked about VFX but I do remember tying it back, and he did have a prosthetic... At times they used a practical prop and sometimes they used a green screen. We flew to London and met with John. It was incredible—*John Hurt*, you know? All the cast had many multiples of costumes, so we had to make an original—a prototype—and at the sitting, we'd tweak it and adjust it and from there go into making the multiples and age it. Ageing was a huge process on *Snowpiercer*—ageing and dying. For fitting John Hurt, everything was pretty tattered. There were a lot of layers, and some of the research was from street people in India, and older men in India, so John responded well to that. He looked at the costume material and said with his great voice, 'Beat it to within an inch of its life, Catherine. Beat it.' So I went back to our ager/dyer and said, 'This is the challenge. John Hurt has challenged you.' And he was very happy with how it came out."

Hurt is quoted as saying, "What I am now, the man, the actor, is a blend of all that has happened," (*The Guardian*, 27 January 2017). This could equally describe Gilliam as John Hurt himself. For the cast and crew of *Snowpiercer*, having him on set was an inspiration but also simply fun.

"John was very nimble and athletic. He was great to work with. He's a history book himself," remembers VFX designer and VFX producer Eric Durst. "One of my greatest experiences in Prague was when I was walking down a little narrow street and I walked past where I knew John lived. I was thinking of him and as I was, the figure that was coming down the road came into view and it was John. I said, 'Hey John,' and he says, 'Oh hey.' Then he puts his arm around me and says, 'Let's go to the pub and have a drink!' He was always doing that. I spent about two hours with John, just talking about his experiences from *Elephant Man* to *Alien* to whatever—it was just such a privilege. The great thing about movies is you get these extraordinary opportunities to have moments with these icons and talk with them and they are very open. It's really cool. He was wonderful to have around."

THIS SPREAD "I didn't really have John Hurt in mind while writing the script, but he was definitely one of the top three or four candidates I had in mind for the character. I don't know why but I really thought a lot about British actors for that role." —Bong Joon Ho
ABOVE "That execution scene we actually shot on the last day when John was on set, so I remember in particular that was the last moment I saw him as an actor on set." —Bong Joon Ho

GREY

In the screenplay, Grey is described as "a lean, muscular young man." On-screen, played by Luke Pasqualino, he seems almost superhuman—leaping across the screen and slicing through the crowded populace. In a film that is all about momentum, Grey is pure physicality.

"Like Yona," Director Bong explains, "Grey is essentially a 'train baby.' Yona is seventeen, she was born on the train, which has been running for seventeen years. Grey is a bit older, maybe twenty-one or twenty-two, and he was two or three when he first got on the train. He, too, has no memory of the outside world, of walking on the ground. He is of the generation who grew up inside the train. This train generation, because they lived under such specific conditions, developed particular qualities, overdeveloped in some areas and devolved in others.

"Curtis asks Yona if she's clairvoyant, but actually she isn't. Her hearing and sense of smell is exceptional, so she can sense what is occurring in the next train car. Living on a train, basically a hermetically sealed box, with its divided sections and cramped and narrow spaces, she's developed the ability to sense and feel what's going on without seeing.

"Similarly, Grey grew up in the confined tail section and learned to move through that environment efficiently. We discussed parkour and how Grey jumps and maneuvers around tight spaces, almost like a wild animal. And so with this skill, he takes on the role of Gilliam's special bodyguard."

Grey is one of the greatest assets the rebels have as they proceed out of the tail section. An efficient and formidable fighter, he lets his actions do the talking for him. "I'm not sure why I made him mute," says Bong Joon Ho. "Grey can hear but cannot speak.

He's covered in tattoos of basic words—'Surrender,' for example—and points at them to communicate."

In order to accurately portray the enigmatic Grey and imbue his movement with such confidence and surety, Pasqualino underwent training with stunt coordinator Julian Spencer.

"Luke didn't have a lot of experience doing action," continues Director Bong, "but he worked diligently with Julian and really pulled off the physicality of the character. And I thought Luke did a good job expressing the solitary and lonely aspect of the character who doesn't seem to communicate with anyone but Gilliam."

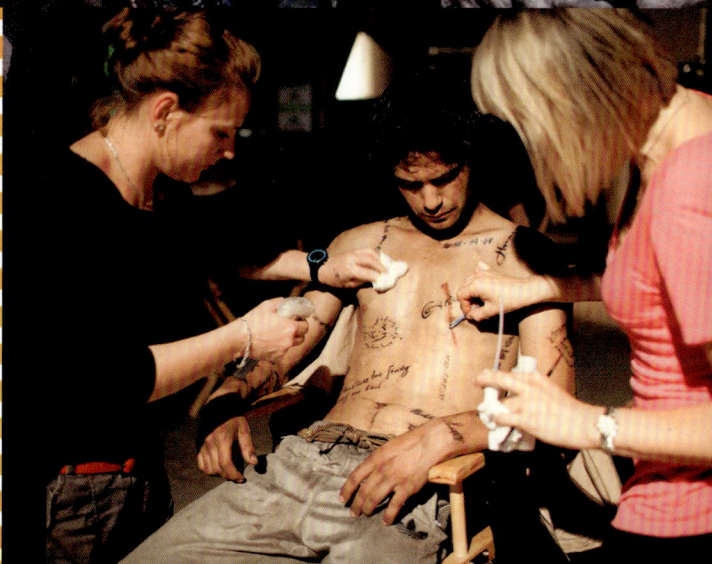

FAR LEFT Rehearsing the sauna fight scene with Vlad Ivanov (Franco the Elder).
LEFT Applying signs of battle and bloodshed to Luke Pasqualino.
ABOVE "We added in the wheelchair section because we thought it might be difficult for John to continue walking on a crutch, so we put him in a wheelchair and had Luke push him around so he would be as comfortable as possible."
—Bong Joon Ho

TANYA

Wilford's assistant, Claude, stands flanked by armed guards, calling children forth and using a tape measure to gauge their suitability for a task we won't discover until the closing minutes of the film. Her decision to take Andrew's son, Andy, and Timmy will have ramifications throughout the story. Timmy's mother is Tanya, played by Oscar®-winner Octavia Spencer.

It was the attraction of working with Bong Joon Ho that brought Spencer to the project, following the similarly politically charged *Fruitvale Station*, also released in 2013.

RIGHT Tanya embraces her son Timmy for what may be the last time.
OPPOSITE LEFT Spencer and Director Bong between takes on the aquarium set.

"I'D SEEN DIRECTOR BONG'S FILMS *THE HOST*, AND *MOTHER* AND KNEW HE WAS A VISIONARY."

OCTAVIA SPENCER

"I'd seen Director Bong's films *The Host*, and *Mother* and knew he was a visionary," recalls Spencer. "That coupled with the synopsis of *Snowpiercer*, and I was completely intrigued. Director Bong had an iPad and basically showed me his vision visually. I went in as myself, made-up, dressed to impress. But, this was a post-apocalyptic film. I remember he just smiled and stared at me for the entire presentation. At the end of our meeting, I realized he was thinking I might not be right for Tanya, so I took off my wig. We laughed hysterically and, later, I found out I got the part."

Tonya

While Director Bong did not write the part of Tanya with any actor in mind, he does storyboard in advance, so had some preconceived notions of what he was looking for. Spencer confirms she had to work to make the part her own, "The makeup and costumes were integral to bringing Tanya to life. Remember, when I met Director Bong, he had the image of Tanya in his mind. I had to show him that I could go there."

'Going there' meant both a tough emotional arc and also embodying the role physically. In the brutal axe fight, Spencer was in the thick of it, as Tanya, weapon in hand, unleashes all the years of injustice and frustration en route to rescuing Timmy. But the actual fight sequence itself was a challenge, pushing Spencer out of her comfort zone.

"Shooting action scenes were scary for me. I was afraid of hitting someone and terrified of being hit accidentally."

Stunt coordinator Julian Spencer helped prepare Octavia for the axe fight, making sure Tanya had her moment and that her character has as much of a reason to be in the fight as anyone else. Essential to this was making it realistic, ensuring that Octavia, and therefore Tanya, fought in line with her own temperament and physicality.

"Octavia couldn't fight at all," he explains. "She didn't have a single angry bone in her body, but I put a little sequence together for her to turn her ability as a human being into her character, rather than get a stunt woman in to double for her, which you see so many times. Suddenly, this lady becomes this ninja warrior—that doesn't work for me. I much prefer to work with the actors than stunt doubles and get them to work with a sequence that is tailored to their own personal body, their ability, and their character. She loved doing that. She had very little to do, but after what scenes we did do together, she just said, 'Fantastic.'"

Despite her struggles, her determination, her fighting, Tanya ultimately does not see the outcome. The elder Franco shoots her in the sauna car and she dies not seeing the revolution succeed or Timmy rescued. However, Spencer feels Tanya was able to make peace with that. "Tanya was a fighter. She knew that in order for her son to have a chance at a meaningful life, she had to fight to secure his future. She died knowing that Curtis would look after her son."

THIS SPREAD Tanya and her son, Timmy, played by Marcanthonee Reis.

ANDREW

Of the ragtag, makeshift army fighting their way to the front, Andrew has his own reasons beyond revolution for joining up. In the opening act, his son, Andy, is taken from him along with Tanya's boy, Timmy.

Andrew is played by actor Ewen Bremner, perhaps most famously known for *Trainspotting* (1996), *Julien Donkey-Boy* (1999), *Black Hawk Down* (2001), and *Wonder Woman* (2017). He credits his agent with getting him involved with *Snowpiercer*. "He was already a huge Bong Joon Ho freak and said, 'You've got to go and meet him, you've got to, got to,

got to go and meet him...'" and Bremner quickly found himself as part of the Bong Joon Ho 'family.'

"Everybody just kind of fell in love with [Director Bong]," Bremner says. "It was like a real warm glow, not just on set but off set as well. It was an unusually warm experience making that film... There's something about him—everyone just wants to reach out and do their best for him, and help. I've worked with a few directors like that in my time as an actor, but it's a little bit uncommon how connected people feel to him."

This warmth and essential humanity enables a film that could have been more objective and cynical to be powered as much by emotion as politics.

"He's a sensitive guy. He has a vulnerability about him that makes him very honest and which he doesn't try to hide. A lot of directors kind of build some sort of defensive armor around themselves because of the position they hold and the things you're going to want from them—the gauntlet they have to run when they release a film to the world, critically, and being responsible for their film. But Bong has retained a real natural vulnerability that he doesn't try to cover up and hide, and that's really engaging and endearing to everyone that works with him... In so many of his films, you see that he's kind of looking into the abyss of the side of humanity that is scary—the side we look away from, the side we don't want to see—and he's brave in the way that he turns his gaze to that. He doesn't do it in a cynical way, or a sensationalist way, he does it in a generous way—in the name of honesty."

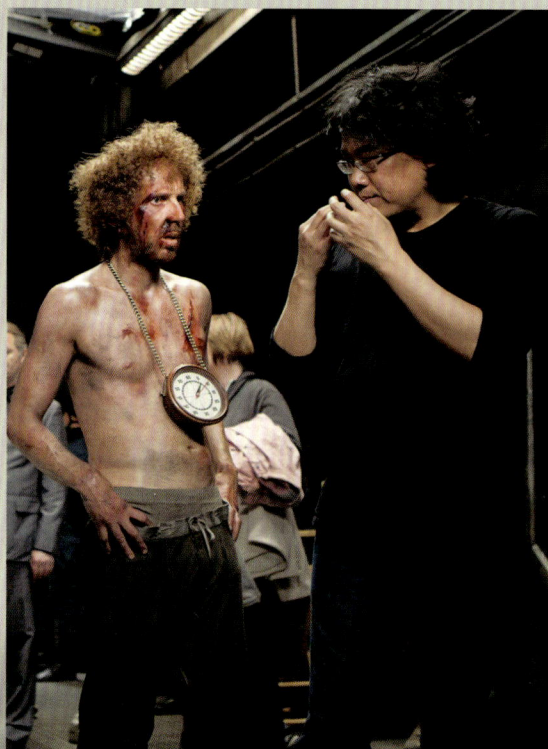

"I ASKED THE ARTIST TO COME UP WITH THAT ARTWORK [ABOVE]. IT WAS KIND OF LIKE A STORYBOARD. IT WAS ALMOST CLOSER TO BEING BLACK AND WHITE RATHER THAN BEING COLOR. OUT OF ALL THE PAINTINGS THAT HE DID, THAT ONE IN PARTICULAR HAD THAT VERY PRIMITIVE FEELING."

BONG JOON HO

THIS SPREAD "To have that fantastic wig and all of the dirt—all of that was really fun... To make a wig work is not easy, it's such a specialist job." —Ewen Bremner

The character of Andrew in *Snowpiercer* is one of the most emotional and driven of the ensemble. While caught up in this great struggle for power and change, he is most purely just a desperate father, a reference that Bremner explains was "important to Director Bong: fatherhood, that relationship, the protector of your child." Ultimately, it is not a happy ending for Andrew or for his son. They represent just two of countless multitudes who suffer for a cause and never see the eventual outcome in this film.

"Director Bong is not scared to let it be sad, you know? To let the story be tragic. He's not afraid of that. It is very tough for all of these characters. They're in a very tough situation, and that provokes a lot of questions. For me, it's the same in the film *Parasite* (2019). He's showing you a microcosm of society… It forces you to engage with that idea of order versus chaos. In *Snowpiercer*, you want the revolutionaries to become liberated. The upper classes are holding onto order with an iron grip because they know if they release that grip then they lose their lives and their status and everything that makes their lives kind of bearable and superior. Bong is very much enjoying putting that problem in your face. This is a problem that we hide from but cannot escape— order versus chaos. There's nowhere to hide from that in *Snowpiercer* and also, in a slightly different way, in *Parasite*."

NAMGOONG AND YONA

The collaborations between Bong Joon Ho and Song Kang Ho not only showcase one of the greatest director-actor partnerships working today but have also created some of the most fascinating and celebrated films in recent history.

Not a formally trained actor, Song Kang Ho first rose to prominence in 2000's *Joint Security Area*, winning a (shared) Best Actor trophy at the Busan Film Critics Awards for his performance. That film was also a turning point for its director, Park Chan-wook, the South Korean filmmaker whose films such as the 'Vengeance trilogy' and *The Handmaiden* (2016) have confirmed him as one of the best directors in the world. Park Chan-wook is one of the producers on *Snowpiercer*.

It was three years after *Joint Security Area* when Song first worked with Bong Joon Ho on the film that would turn out to be the director's breakthrough, *Memories of Murder* (2003). Regarded as a classic of the crime drama genre, both filmmaker and actor found a rhythm that has carried through into each of their projects together, despite the vastly different genres and characterizations of each: *The Host*, *Snowpiercer*, and *Parasite*.

"THEY'RE ACTORS THAT I LOVE VERY MUCH."

BONG JOON HO

In *Snowpiercer*, Song Kang Ho's character, Namgoong, is key to the plot, both figuratively and literally. He is brought into the rebellion—freed from his incarceration—because, as a security technician, he is the only one who can unlock the train-car doors. However, as the film continues, he becomes the main supporting player and his actions have as much of an impact on the story as those of Curtis.

To join the rebellion, he has two conditions: they must supply him with lumps of kronole—a drug that he appears to be addicted to—and they must also free his daughter, Yona, who has been similarly incarcerated.

OPPOSITE LEFT Director Bong and Song Kang Ho between takes.
BOTTOM RIGHT Preparing to shoot Namgoong's cinematic entrance via his exit from imprisonment.

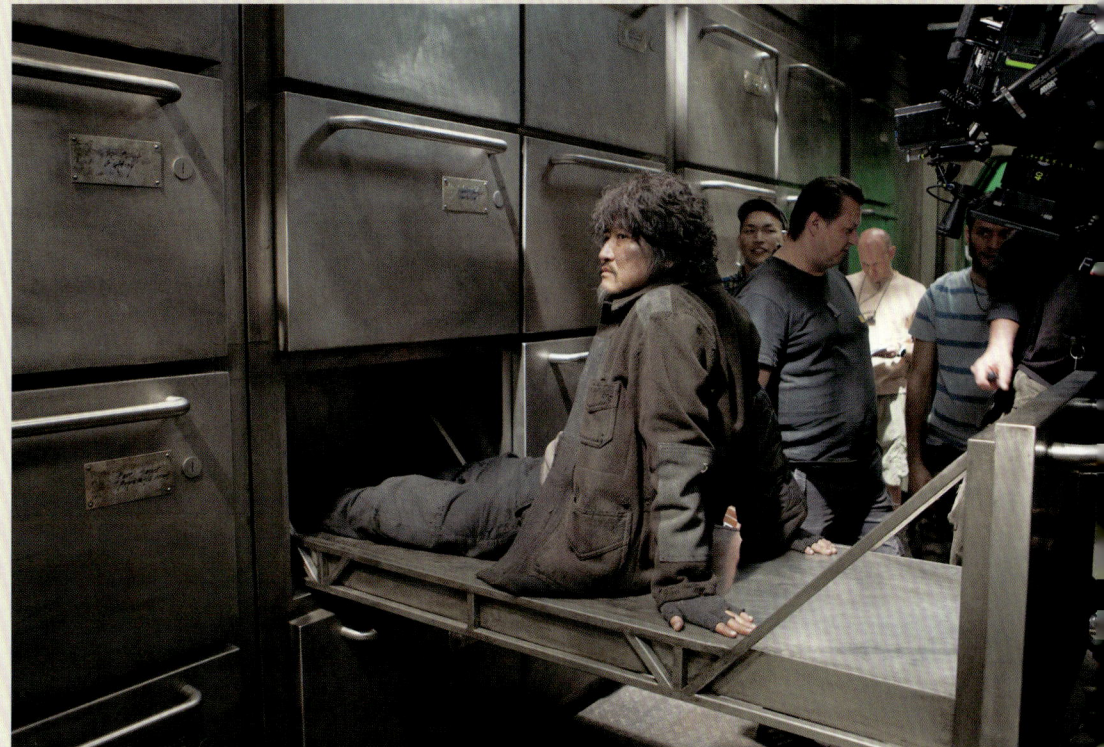

"YOU COULD SAY THAT
WHEN I CONCEIVED OF
THIS FILM, IT REALLY BEGAN
WITH YONA AND ENDED
WITH HER AS WELL."

BONG JOON HO

Yona is played by Ko Asung, who had previously worked with Bong Joon Ho on *The Host*. Even though it is a very different role and different film, there are links between the character of Park Hyun Seo in *The Host* and Yona. To some degree, both act as the audience's avatars on-screen, as we learn so much about the worlds we are seeing through their eyes, and both movies ultimately concern themselves with the salvation of Park and Yona.

Yona was born on the train and has never known anything but the Snowpiercer. It is Yona's character that highlights the strength of *Snowpiercer*'s screenplay. Much of the context and exposition that we need to know as an audience—and which will prove vital later—is delivered as Namgoong explains to Yona key events from the last seventeen years and essential information, such as what soil is and the type of snow that is falling on the windows. It is Namgoong and Yona who are looking sideways, out of the windows into the world, while Curtis and his followers only look forward. Their concern is the future of the train; Namgoong and Yona are more interested in a future outside of the train.

LEFT Ko Asung taking it easy on set.
OPPOSITE BOTTOM LEFT Director Bong and Ko in discussion during a pause between camera rolls.
OPPOSITE BOTTOM RIGHT A photo from the first day of shooting, with Ko the only principal actor to be on the production that early.

It is Yona's intervention that the film hinges on. Just when it seems as if Curtis is going to accept Wilford's offer to take his mantle, Yona levers open a panel in the floor to reveal the abducted children working in the hellish depths of the engine: unthinking cogs in the machine of capitalism. She reminds Curtis of the value of humanity. While he has been so occupied with moving forward in the traditional linear fashion that ultimately plays right into Wilford's plan, Yona has been looking left and right to the outside and finally downward. She and Namgoong have realized there must be another way to progress—an alternative direction.

We have watched Curtis throughout the film in profile choosing left or right. As the film ends and Yona sets foot on solid ground, she is face-on, walking straight toward the camera. She is making her own path in the snow.

"The thing that I talked about with Ko Asung is that Yona is like a new spread of humanity," explains Bong Joon Ho. "She's a train baby that was born on the train; she's seventeen years old, which is the number of years the train's been running, and all the other adult characters have experienced life on earth but Yona hasn't. In one of the versions of the script, the first page starts with a voiceover from Yona. The voice goes, 'I started rattling from the moment I was born, because I was born on a running train,' and we ended up taking this out of subsequent versions. But the film also ends with Yona and Timmy escaping the train, so you could say that when I conceived of this film, it really began with Yona and ended with her as well."

THE DIVINE KEEPER OF THE SACRED ENGINE:

WILFORD

It's the climax of the film. Curtis has finally made it to the front. All the bloodshed and sacrifice has come to this: the sacred engine, with its divine leader, Wilford. However, what we find when Curtis steps through the door is not divinity, not even a leader. Wilford is just a man.

"Director Bong wanted it to be a bit of a surprise with this man who was in charge of this whole situation, whose idea it was," explains legendary actor Ed Harris, who assumes the role of Wilford, the 'man behind the curtain.' "He was not some kind of overbearing, loud, commanding person, but had a certain calmness and confidence about him; a stillness. He wielded his power somewhat quietly."

In *Le Transperceneige*, the engineer maintaining the train is Alec Forrester, a frail, hermit of a man, paranoid, terminally ill, and who passes the caretaking of the engine over to Proloff, the protagonist. We see more of Wilford's worldview than we do of Forrester's in the film. If Forrester is mad, it's due to the insane situation and claustrophobia; if Wilford is mad then he always was—being the type of man who would build such a machine and make himself lord of it. He's not even 'driving' the train. And a train without a driver will sooner or later go off the rails.

"You've got certain limitations when you've got X amount of space to hold X number of people," explains Harris. "You've got a class structure that isn't exactly humane. I don't know about 'evil,' but I don't know what the word would be—'hypocrisy' perhaps... In this business, you meet a lot of people with power and you see how they wield it differently. I don't remember anyone I thought of specifically, but there are a lot of men I've come across who had certain qualities: untouchable power and self-confidence. Self-righteousness, almost. People that you don't really enjoy being around, because it's always on their terms. There's a bit of Christof [referring to his character in 1998's *The Truman Show*] in there for sure. The lack of any kind of sensitivity or lack of feeling or concern about the people that are being harmed. He's saying, 'That's the way it is, that's the way it has to be.'

Le Transperceneige, Jacques Lob and Jean-Marc Rochette © CASTERMAN

There's no guilt or fear of any recrimination. I'm God and you're not."

We find him cooking a steak, wearing a beautiful robe, with a slightly bemused look on his face. "You did a man's work," he says to Curtis, reminiscent of the famous line spoken by Gaff in the penultimate scene in Blade Runner (1982). There is a surety, an attractiveness about him, that makes his offer to Curtis so very tempting.

Ed Harris was brought on quite late to the project. Given the shooting had been almost chronological to the film's plot, the Wilford scenes were some of the last to be shot. On the one hand, it meant they had been able to decide in advance on Wilford's costume, but on the other, Harris had to quickly figure out who this man was and his mentality. Costume designer Catherine George says, "It was a very quick fitting, and I remember Ed Harris coming in. Usually you have a rack full of clothes that you can play around with, but this was basically three robes and a pair of pyjamas— that's it!

"I did a lot of research. We talked a lot about Wilford and who he was. Someone with that much power doesn't have to impress anyone and is so isolated. Luxury and comfort: we wanted to give off that impression. I showed Director Bong a picture of Julian Schnabel in his pyjamas and his robe while he was showing some of his art to someone. I mean, he wears them out on the street and stuff, and so it had the right mood: someone so confident and can do what they want. It seemed to fit well, so we kind of went down that road. The fabric and the prints were camera tested and worked out well on the set, and he's got his own Wilford slippers. We figured this is stuff that's probably been on the train for a while so we aged it a little bit, but in a subtle way."

CHAPTER THREE:

DESIGNING THE FILM

One of Bong Joon Ho's many strengths as a director is his visual storytelling and just how much he can communicate through his compositions—both in the final frames and on paper in preproduction. When pitching the film to studios and to the crew, Director Bong would present the concept art he had created, which showed the look, tone, and scale he was aiming for. Tellingly, he did not show people the original graphic novel, which, one would think, would seem like a ready-made reference for the film. The art he brought to meetings showed *his* version of *Snowpiercer* and the world he was creating.

VFX designer and VFX producer Eric Durst explains Director Bong's process: "I met him for the first time 2 July, 2011. He presented—as he does many people—a series of illustrations that show what the film is. He's very visual or uses his visual material to explain a lot of what he's thought about. A good part of that meeting was him showing what he had done, and I showed him what I had done. I guess we hit it off and worked it out. The first meeting I had with him in Prague, he laid out some of the material he had before but some other material this time. He had five or seven images and he said, 'Eric, this is the film. This is the train, this is what the interior looks like.' It had the vibe and the whole essence of the film in just these few images. I had a few questions and that was it. It was like a fifteen-minute meeting. I was very impressed with that because I got so much material or feeling of the movie in just that short amount of time."

Slow Track In

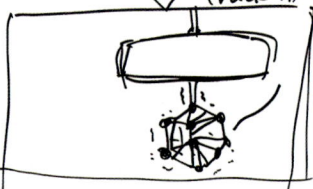

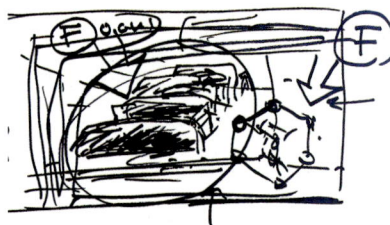

MIRROR

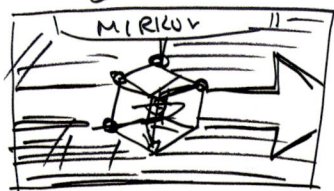

Light →

90°
Pan

Right

"Save The Plant"

THIS PAGE "The thing I remember most is walking into that sound stage and seeing this board with all the shots planned out. They would do a shot and it would be crossed out and then they'd go on to the next one, and the editor was sitting right there, cutting as it was being shot. That's something I will always remember, just the nature of the shoot." —Ed Harris

When Bong Joon Ho steps on set, he is sure of what he is going to shoot and how he is going to shoot it. These are, of course, not random choices. He has thought through every shot of the film and the visual story that is being told—how each shot relates to the next, a constant catalytic evolution throughout the running time. As preordained as it is that a train must eventually reach its destination, so the first shot of a Bong Joon Ho film inevitably leads to the final shot.

Eric Durst continues, "I went back to my office and opened a folder that I had found on our shared server and went through all the folders of the images that had been created for the film up to that point. I saw there were hundreds and hundreds and hundreds of images and that he had distilled everything down to these seven images, and that's how he works. He's able to take all the possibilities that you could do in a film—you could shoot it a thousand different ways, interpret it a number of different ways—and he's looked at all the viewpoints, made decisions, and then consolidated it down. That's why he's so clear about it. And that's why he's so open on the set. You can ask him anything at all and he doesn't have any vibe of *I'm the director, shut up, just do your job*. There's none of that. He talks about how he's in control all the time, and he *is* in control, but he's in control because he just knows more. He's done his homework and he'll answer any question you have because he's already thought about it and he's already considered why that doesn't work or why part of that works or why this other option works. He can give you a very succinct answer on that. It's really remarkable to work with somebody like that."

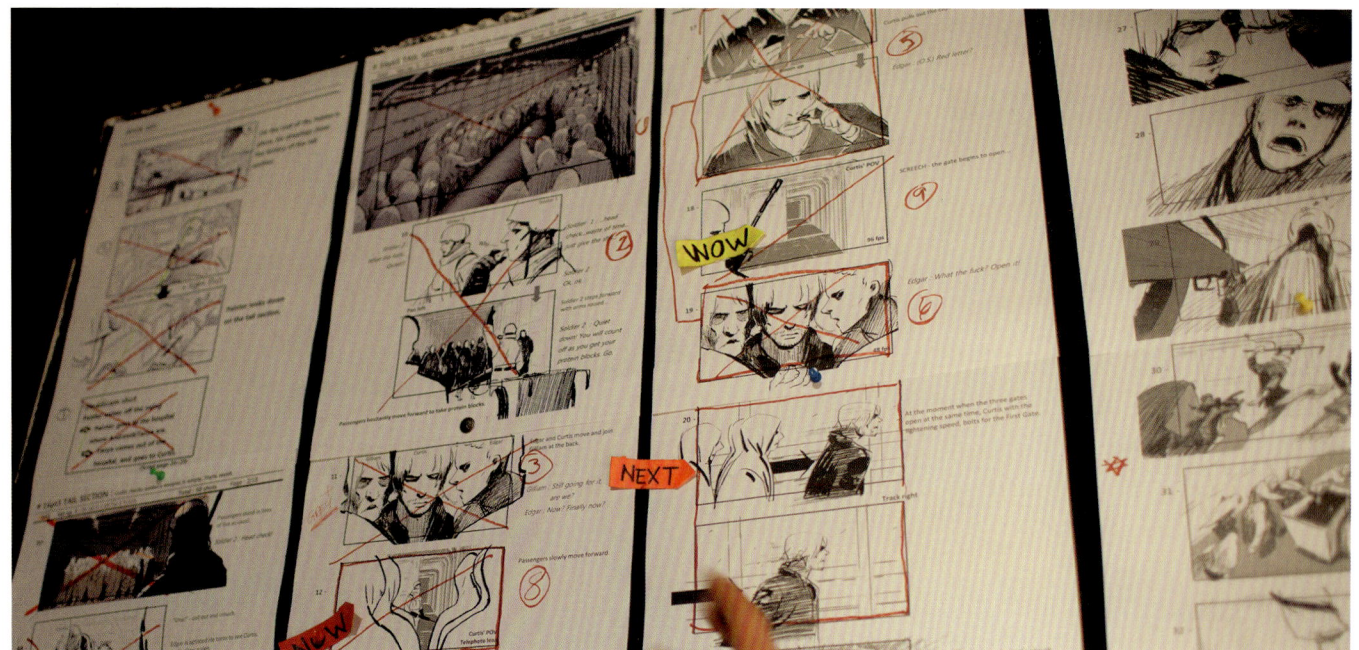

It's a sentiment echoed by Jamie Bell, showing how Director Bong's specificity relates to acting and people as much as shot design. "It was very clear very quickly that this was going to be unlike any film experience I'd ever had, just in terms of construction of scenes, how you get through scenes, coverage of scenes, how action is told to you, what you're expected to do, the narrative journey of the scene you're expected to follow and understand. I've never seen anyone more prepared than Bong, that's what I'm trying to say. Never in my life... I've never seen someone do a finite detail look at a storyboard, or a wall of storyboards and go, 'This bit now, this line now, this way you hold your hand out.' He is precise to the small physical gesture."

It is well-publicized that Director Bong storyboards all of his films—with a whole book dedicated to his *Parasite* (2019) imagery—and the pieces he and other artists draw are both descriptive and prescriptive. In their framing, angle, and composition, they say exactly what Director Bong is looking to shoot. It's well-known that during meetings, Sir Ridley Scott will grab a pencil and blank sheet of paper and start drawing an idea he has or something he wants to explain through an image. Similarly, Bong Joon Ho is able to let a picture do the talking—a picture that expresses an idea he has been working on for weeks, if not months. His movies are crafted and every moment of them has his fingerprints on.

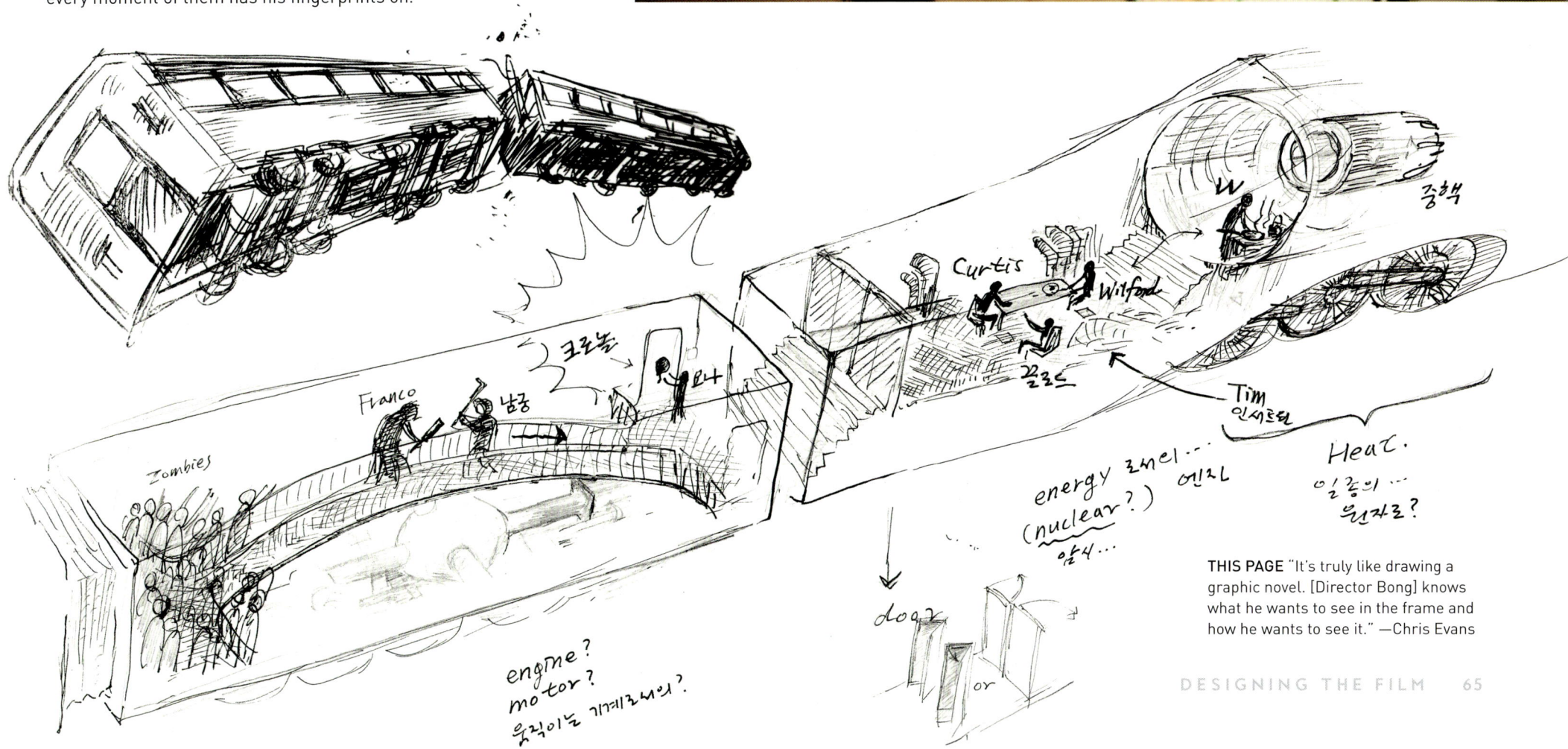

THIS PAGE "It's truly like drawing a graphic novel. [Director Bong] knows what he wants to see in the frame and how he wants to see it." —Chris Evans

 # 3 TAIL SECTION :   Tail Section line up for rationing. Edgar reveals his frustration to Curtis.

| DAY | Set up. 1 : 04 Tail D + 05 Tail E PLAZA | Total : 25 shots | Page: 1/13 |

 # 3 TAIL SECTION :   Tail Section line up for rationing. Edgar reveals his frustration to Curtis.

| DAY | Set up. 1 : 04 Tail D + 05 Tail E PLAZA | Total : 25 shots | Page: 1/13 |

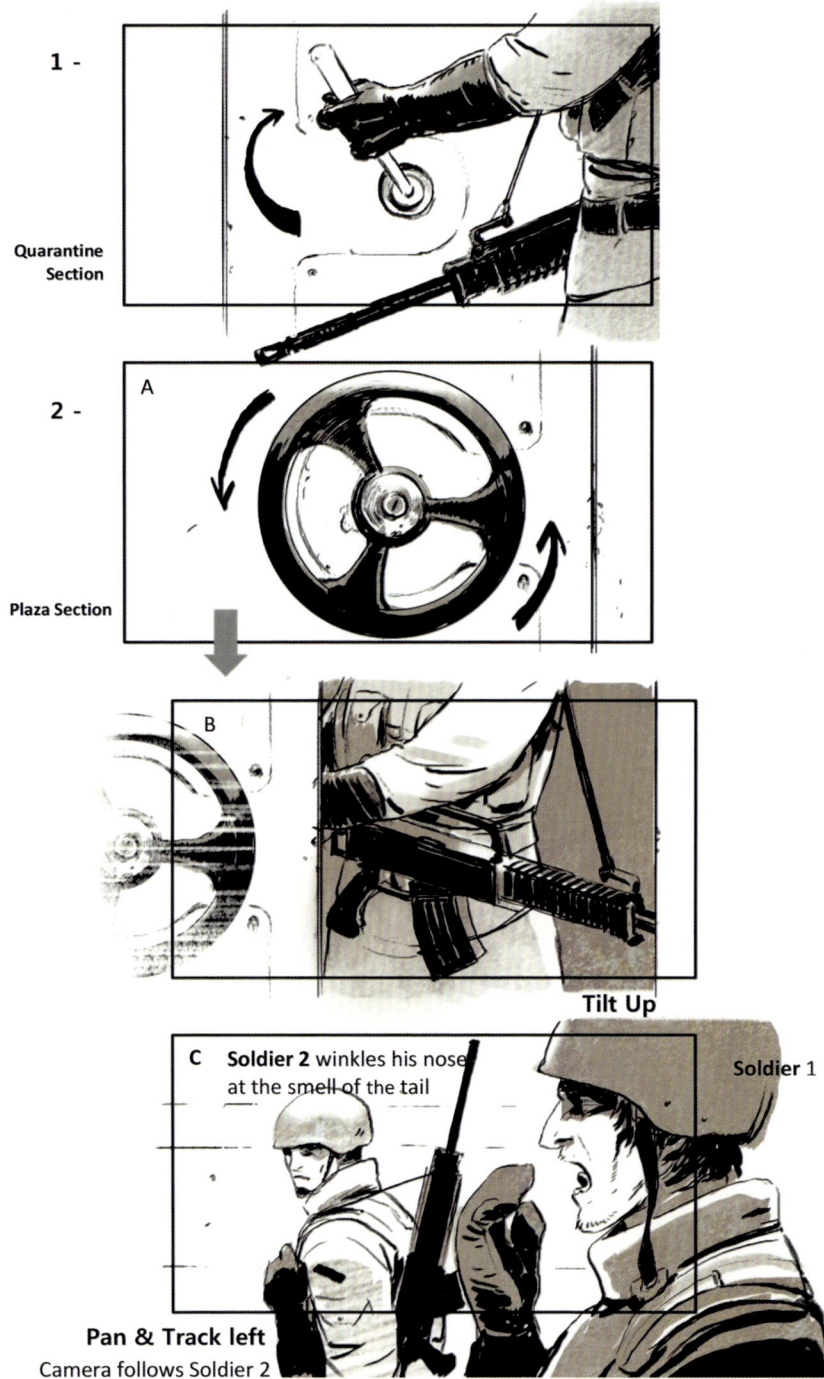

"I'VE NEVER SEEN ANYONE MORE PREPARED THAN BONG, THAT'S WHAT I'M TRYING TO SAY. NEVER IN MY LIFE..."

JAMIE BELL

3 -

Curtis' fingers count 2 - 3 - 4...

Edgar : Curtis - sit down.

4 -

Curtis stares past the iron gate.

Edgar : (O.S.) sit down.

5 -

Soldier 2

Soldier 1

Soldier 2 : I said sit down!

6 -

Curtis does not budge an inch.

7-

8 -

Curtis sits suddenly.

9 -

Edgar : What the fuck are you doing?

10 -

Curtis' POV

Curtis : Counting.

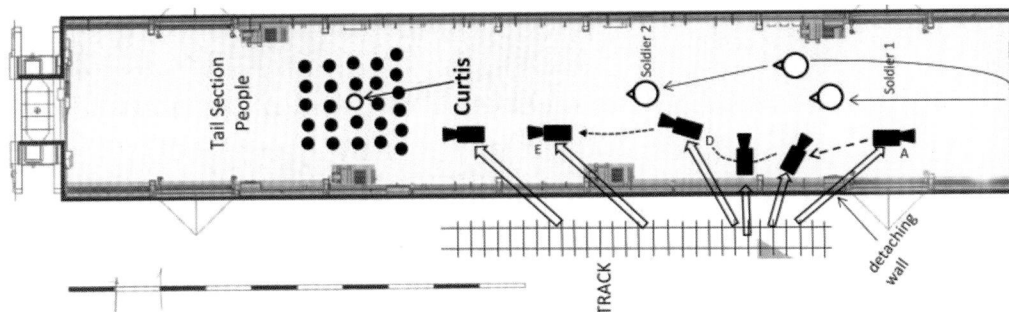

rattling...

rattling...

**Focus moves
Passengers to Gate**

Tail Section
People

Curtis

Soldier 2

Soldier 1

E

D

A

TRACK

detaching
wall

THIS SPREAD Storyboarding the opening scene, including a markedly different-looking Curtis to Chris Evans' eventual on-screen appearance. "[Director Bong] never shoots coverage. It's all according to the storyboards." —Dooho Choi

LEFT An overhead plan of the tail section for blocking and to guide the set build.

"WE WANTED IT TO BE
VERY GLOBAL, NOT JUST
WESTERN. WE WANTED A
VERY GLOBAL INFLUENCE."

CATHERINE GEORGE

"What's great about [Director Bong] is that he spent a lot of time prepping that movie," says production designer Ondřej Nekvasil. "He was always very clear about his ideas. He's always working on simple sketches in his notepads. They are not designs but sketches showing the layout and how things are connected together."

Ondřej Nekvasil was brought up to speed once the production had based itself in Prague and after a great deal of preproduction had already been done. Director Bong's previous production designer was unable to join *Snowpiercer* and it was decided that they needed someone local. Nekvasil had worked on a number of Czechoslovakian film and TV productions, as well as Neil Burger's *The Illusionist* (2006), and had been recommended for the job. When he came on board, the film was already a reality, but the train was not yet on the tracks.

"We got the book of all the concepts and designs that they did in Korea," he explains. "I was really scared because we were starting late. It was early October 2011 and we were supposed to start in February, and I realized that everybody else had been working on the movie since January. They were ten months ahead of us. I was like, *How were we going to get up to speed?* I spoke with the Korean producers and said we need some time for soft prep and we will put all our people together and really get up to the same speed as Director Bong, because otherwise we will have no chance to catch him. He was really ahead. He'd been over everything so many times. It was an important moment. The producers gave us the time and we were able to do the concept work and properly think about the train."

THIS AND PREVIOUS SPREAD There is more to the outside world than just a wall of endless white. Designs such as this show the changes in the geography, color variation, and what signs of civilization are still viewable. It was important that it be Earth— our Earth—covered in snow, not an anonymous land.
BELOW Reminiscent of Pompeii, souls frozen and preserved for eternity.

THE TRAIN

In the script, the train is not overtly described. It is just *there*, without explanation or embellishment. This may be because the script is so propulsive and does not linger over scene-setting. Or it may be a more philosophical choice: the train is there, all around, and it goes without saying—describing it in a screenplay would be as useful as trying to describe Earth. In *Le Transperceneige*, the text box reads, "This is the Snowpiercer, one thousand and one carriages long, carrying the last of civilization through the endless wastes... Its metal hull shelters the survivors of the world that was; those that the white death has condemned to a never-ending journey." The black and white artwork in the *bande dessinée* shows a black, economical cattle train, featureless but for the occasional windows dotted along its sides. It looks like a portable prison.

On his initial phone call meeting to discuss his thoughts on the project, Nekvasil focused not on the aesthetics of the train but the meaning of it. "I'd just got the script two days before," he remembers. "I read part of it but I didn't have the time to read it [in those two days], so I read it overnight before the call. The call was at about 5 a.m. because there was a team in Korea, a team in Los Angeles, and I was in Istanbul, so they had to find the right time for all of us."

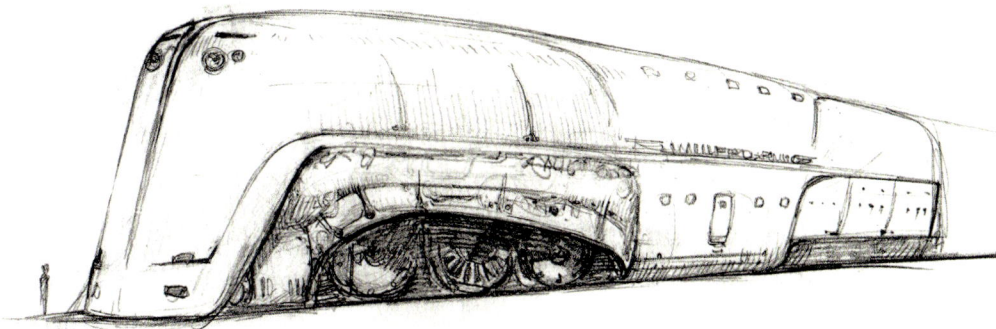

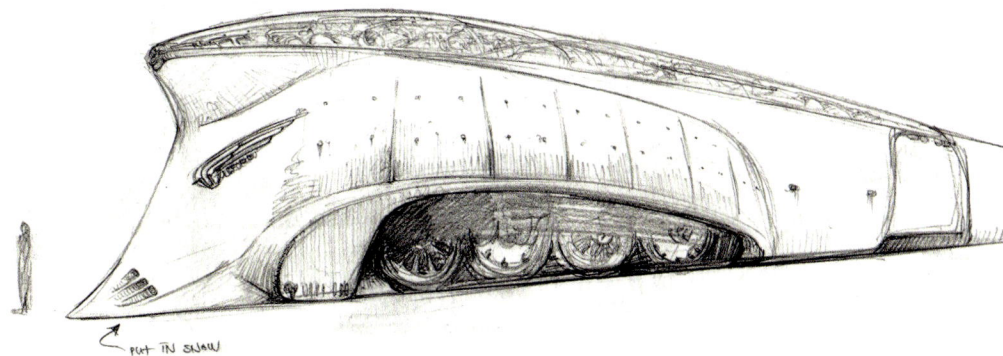

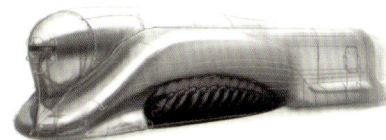

"ONDŘEJ MADE THE WHOLE TRAIN. HE WAS AMAZING.
I WAS VERY LUCKY THAT THE FILM HAD ONDŘEJ AS
THE PRODUCTION DESIGNER. HE WAS SO GREAT."

BONG JOON HO

THIS SPREAD From pencil designs to more finished concept pieces, just eight of the many train artworks. Note the inclusion of characters for scale. "In some of the early sketches, they planned to do a train that would be completely enormous, like huge train cars. I said that I feel that it's not a good direction because everybody has some impression about trains and if it goes too big, it will not be a train. It will be something else." —Ondřej Nekvasil

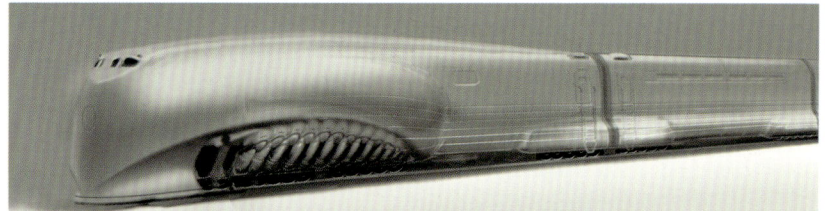

THIS SPREAD A variety of designs from Soviet-style approaches and something more animalistic that resembles a whale through to more obviously industrial machines that seem to run on coal due to the clouds of smoke and steam.

"It was early morning," Nekvasil continues, "and I didn't sleep because I had to read the script. I just remember that I didn't talk about the design at all. I was just talking about the society and about the life behind a fence, because that's my experience of growing up. I grew up behind the Iron Curtain in the Czech Republic and we discussed the situation—a split between the people and the connection between culture and skin tone. Some people are in the position behind the door and some people are in the position at the front of the train, behind that wall. That was our first conversation."

Almost immediately , the train design went in a different direction to that of the graphic novel, which resembles an armored train used by the 'Whites' in the Russian Civil War.

Coming up with a train that looked striking for its own sake was not on the agenda; everything had to have a reason.

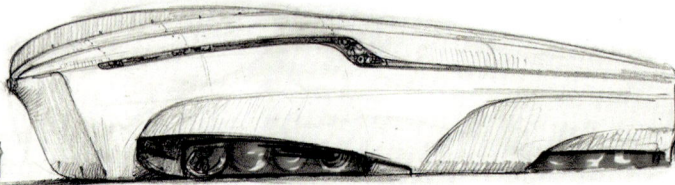

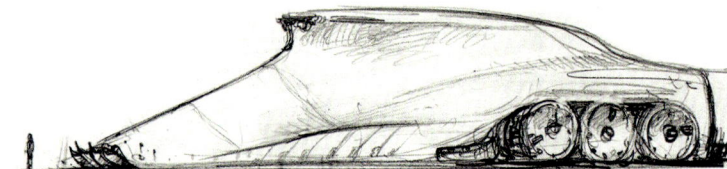

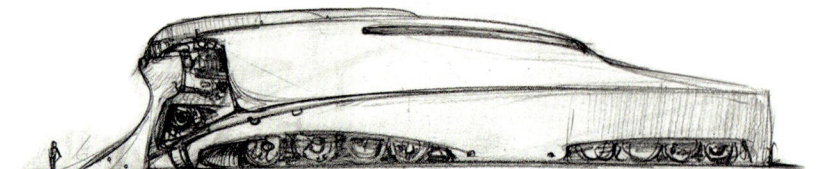

THIS SPREAD "Some cars are contemporary, some aren't and it doesn't look like a completely sci-fi movie for any of us." —Ondřej Nekvasil

GREENHOUSE

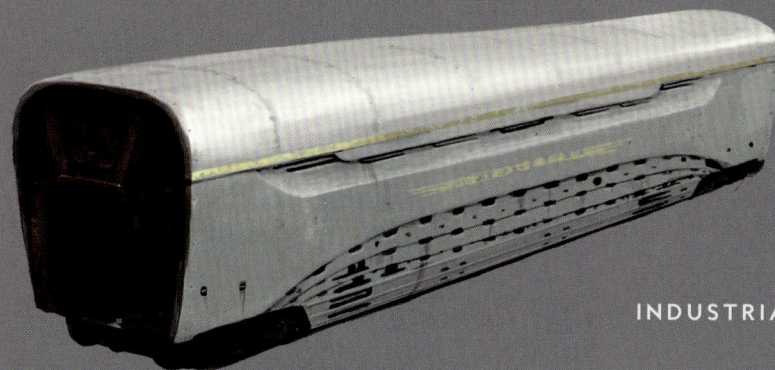

INDUSTRIAL

RESIDENTIAL

SWIMMING POOL

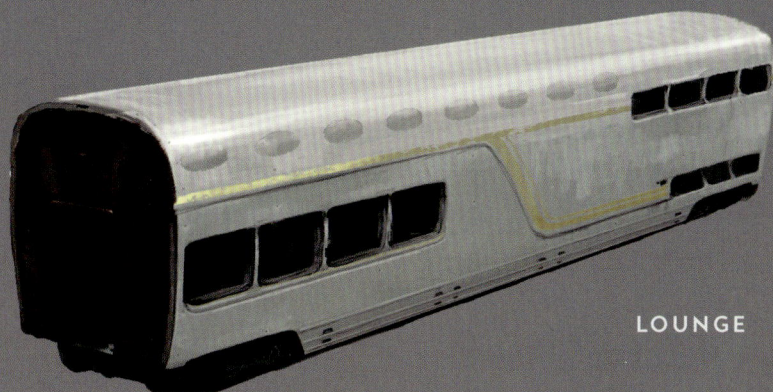

LOUNGE

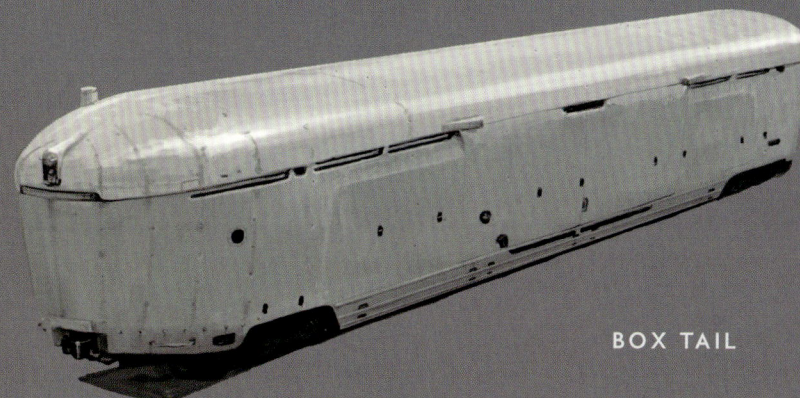

BOX TAIL

Nekvasil explains, "I kind of liked the idea that maybe the train was not a completely designed train, like Japanese bullet trains are one sleek design for the whole train, like it's conceived and realized by one man. I said, 'What about if the train is actually put together with cars that were made in different periods and times? Some of them could be twenty years old, some could be brand new. They put them together because it's a long train, but they were not building that train as one train.'"

Even though the film is high concept, it was essential that it was rooted in reality. It may be set in the future, but the world and people of *Snowpiercer* are as alive and human as any Director Bong has created in his other movies. The story may be post-apocalyptic but in order to be relatable, it has to be recognizable.

"In the original designs, the original concepts, which I got from Korea," recalls Nekvasil, "each car was almost twenty feet wide. The whole train is wider. All the cars were bigger. I said that I don't think it's a good idea. It'll look like a room and not like a train car. People won't buy it. I was really pitching the idea that we had to go back to the standard train car size and we had to find a way to shoot in there but keep the narrowness of the car.

"It has the length and narrowness, the feeling of the corridor of a train car. On a train car, you have that feeling. That was the biggest change we started with: that we have to do it like a normal train. We couldn't build that amazing big train. Later on, when we did the research, we realized that there was a guy before who had a plan to build a train like that—no surprise, it was Adolf Hitler. We found a German book, which was completely about the project of that train, which was supposed to go directly from Berlin or Belsen and was planned for moving the fuel, tanks, and all of that. The rails would be three meters wide and the train would be five meters wide—an enormous train going through Europe."

The production design team's job concerned both the exterior and interior of the train. Each carriage or car the characters pass through tells them more about their situation, their goal, and, more broadly,

about society in general. The cars all have unique styles, offering different looks at the world of the train and its attitudes to class, but also providing bold visual juxtapositions that make the film itself so rich to behold.

"We went through each car using references and designs and we put together the character of each car... Some of them could be a little bit similar but there was always a different concept, a different story behind each car... There's a car like a hospital, there's a car where the people live together, there's a trash car where they have all the trash. All that stuff was quite important for us. I think that first six or seven weeks of the prep were crucial for us because during that time, we were able to define that and really to get to the same level as Director Bong regarding the knowledge of the train. Without that [time], we would be always behind him."

THIS SPREAD "We ended up somewhere between nine to ten feet wide, which is bigger than a normal train but still believable." —Ondřej Nekvasil

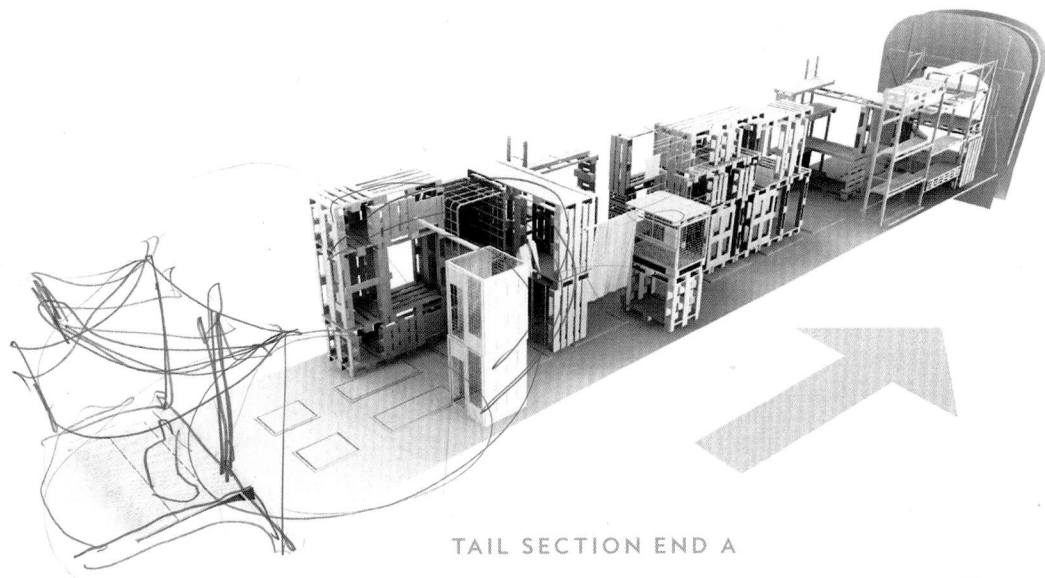
TAIL SECTION END A

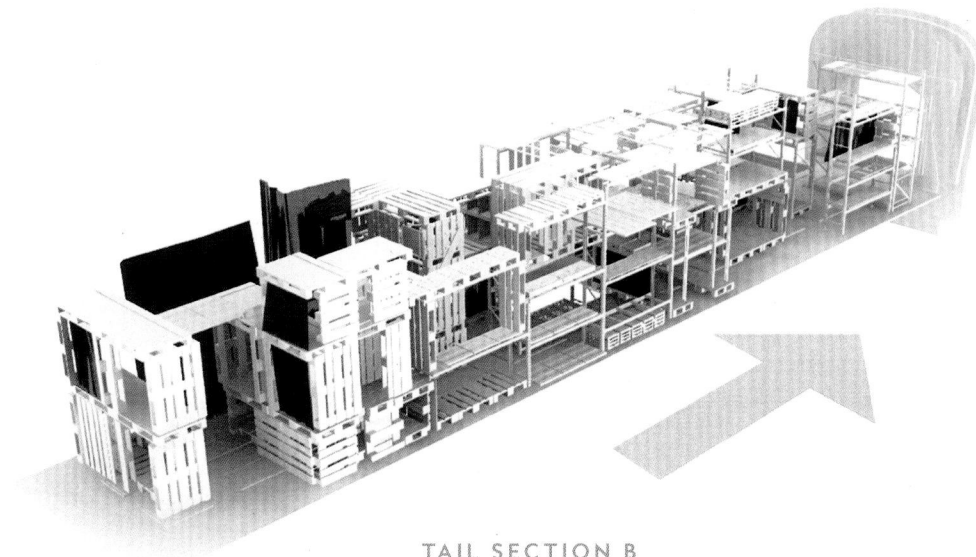
TAIL SECTION B

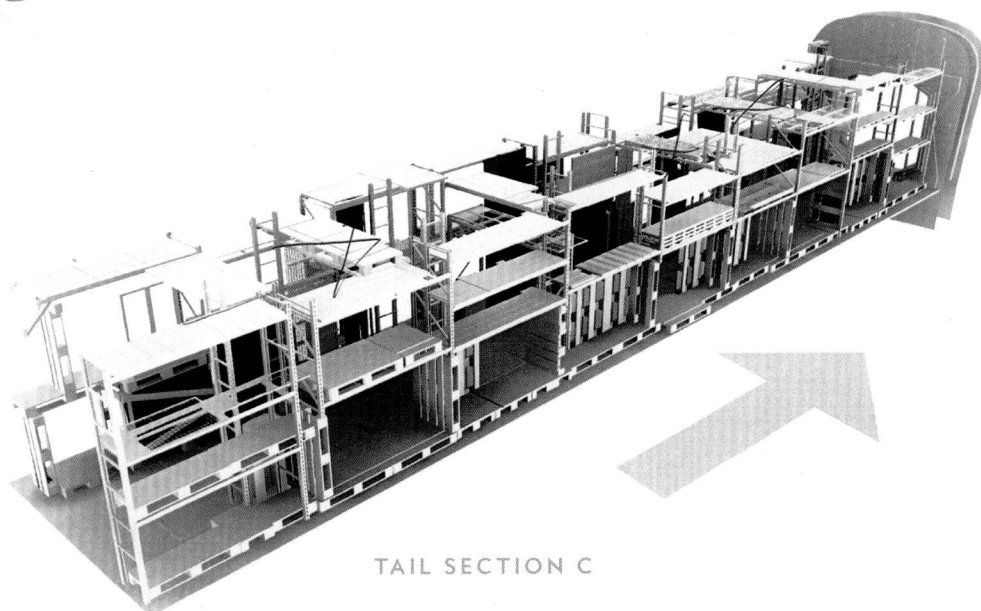
TAIL SECTION C

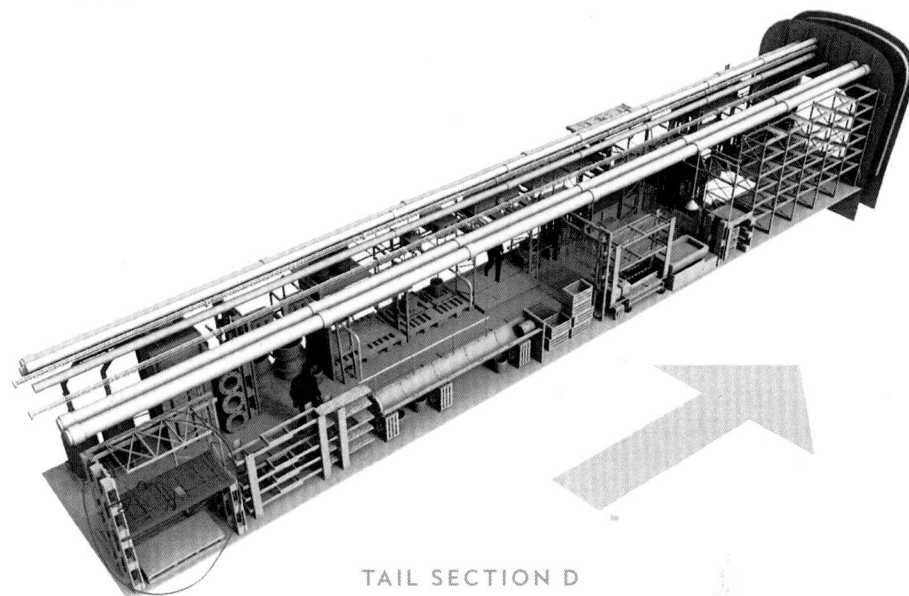
TAIL SECTION D

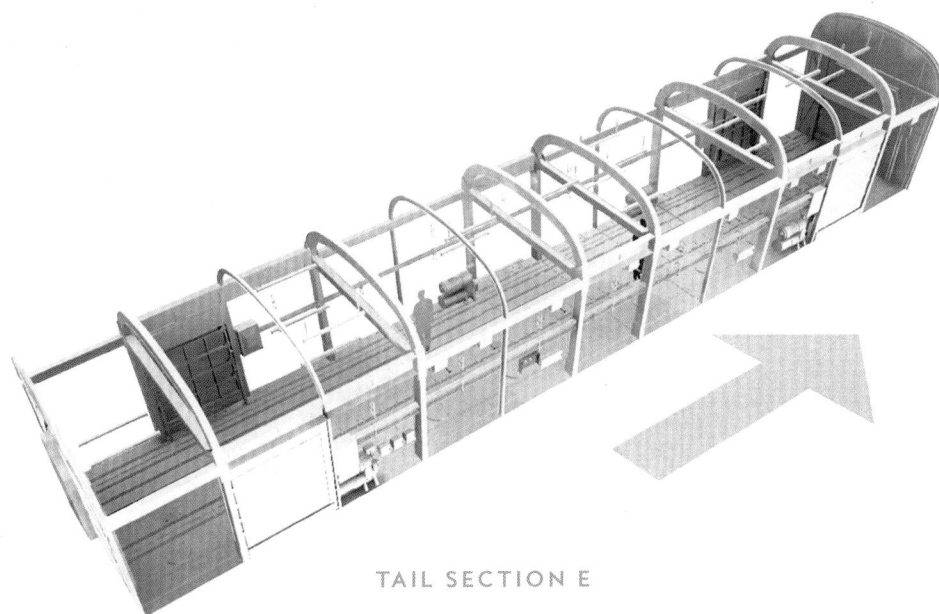
TAIL SECTION E

"The fact that we were able to spend the time together to talk about each car, to talk about each character, was essential. We had a drawer full of pictures and could say: this is not a good one, this is a better direction, etc. With the layout, the basic elements of it, we could put together all the information about the cars. That was really important because after that, we could be focused on the design and we knew already what we were aiming for. It was a constant time pressure—they needed to build these cars."

The train became a quite literal thing for the filmmakers, with personality, life, and death populating it. The Snowpiercer became a home away from home as months were spent detailing every facet of it ahead of finally building the real thing.

CHAPTER FOUR

PIECE BY PIECE

The movie was Bong Joon Ho's first feature film to be shot outside of Korea. While that suited the diverse cast and also the global nature of the movie, the decision was made for practical rather than philosophical reasons.

"Early on, there was a conversation about shooting it in Korea," recalls Dooho Choi. "We looked at places in Canada and the US, but Eastern Europe became the front-runner because there are great tax credits. Director Bong and Guillermo del Toro had gotten to know one another as they were both on the awards circuit at the same time for *The Host* and *Pan's Labyrinth* [2006]. Guillermo had shot *Hellboy* [2004] in the Czech Republic and *Hellboy II: The Golden Army* [2008] in Hungary, so Director Bong wrote to him about the pros and cons of each country. Ultimately, we decided on the Czech Republic.

"The reason for going to Barrandov Studios was because their three biggest sound stages were next to each other and you could open the doors to make it one enormous stage. Most stages are square, but this configuration gave us a long rectangular space, which is what we needed to build a train set. It was very important for Director Bong to sell the realism of being on a train. Part of that was being able to see down through the car and into the next car, to see the curvature as the train was turning; he was adamant about that, and so Prague was the winner."

Despite the enormous space at their disposal, it was still not feasible to build the entire train set. Doing so would have been hugely expensive but also impractical. What the production was able to do was reuse the sets in a cost-effective way that worked with the carefully planned shooting schedule, including which actors were available when.

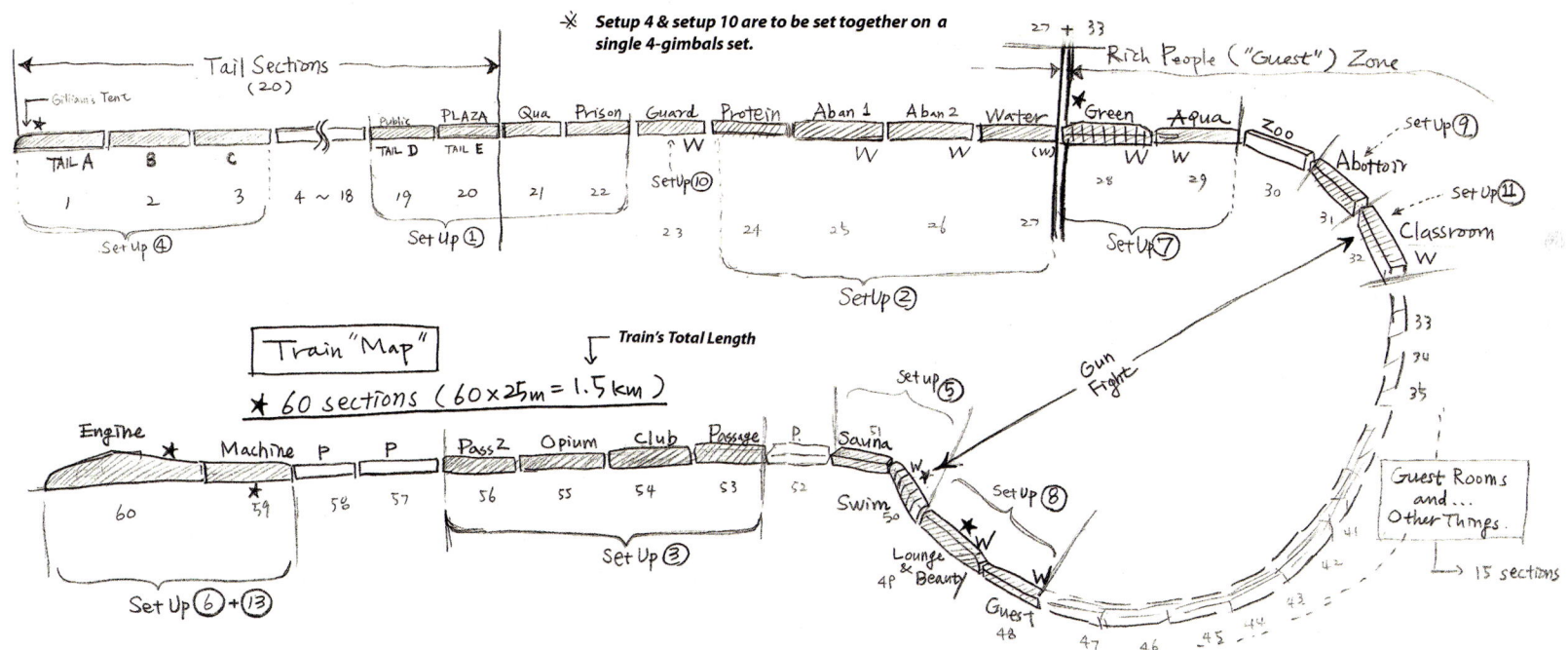

OPPOSITE Building the enormous train set at Barrandov Studios.
ABOVE A train diagram, detailing sixty individual carriages, drawn by Director Bong.

AQUARIUM

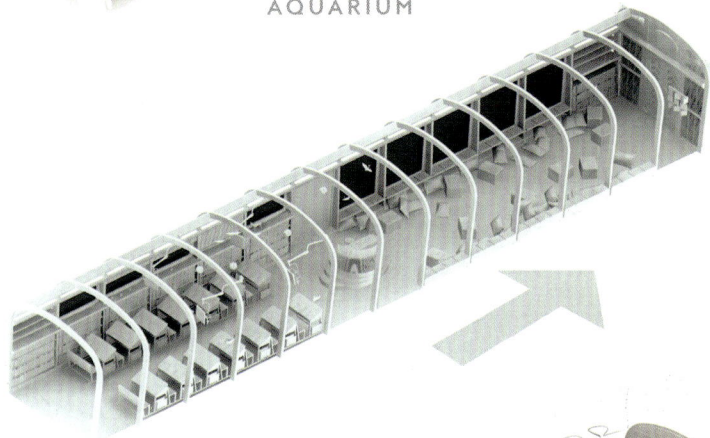

CLASSROOM

LIVING QUARTERS

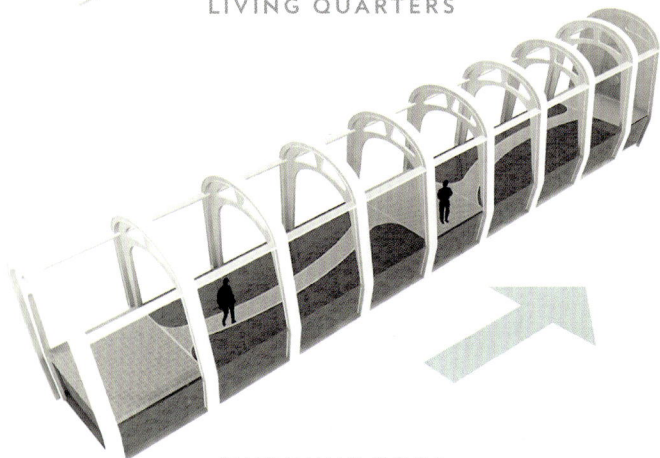

SWIMMING POOL

In the graphic novel, the train is made up of 1001 carriages. The film scaled that down to sixty (see diagram on page 81), though they only built twenty-six—not nearly so many but still a significant number of sets to build. While *Le Transperceneige* mostly uses a uniform look for the carriages until Proloff nears the front—such as the library car, the cannabis car, and the brothel car—the movie version of the Snowpiercer has an entirely different venue in every car. Each one tells us something about the world and politics of the train, and offers something to our protagonists either in the form of information or danger.

Even though twenty-six cars in total were built over the duration of the shoot, there was only a maximum of four in use at any one time. The production created a cycle of making, shooting, then breaking apart a set, which was only able to happen because of the months of preparation and the ability of all departments to work together on schedule, with the goal of realizing Director Bong's precise vision.

Many of Director Bong's movies revel in subverting expectations and toying with genres and concepts. Despite the post-apocalyptic trappings of *Snowpiercer* that automatically categorize it as a 'sci-fi film,' it is really at its core a single-location thriller, like *Rope* (1948), *12 Angry Men* (1957), *Rear Window* (1954), or *Panic Room* (2002). It just so happens that Director Bong's single location is stretched out over twenty-six different train cars.

"This film really, throughout the entire running time, all happens within this one train and I think that premise really excited me and that's why I decided to adapt this graphic novel into a film," says Bong Joon Ho. "A train is pretty simple, it's just a narrow and long straight line. But once the shooting days came closer, I started getting really scared, thinking about how I was going to pull this off. The director of photograpy and I had a lot of conversations about this and we teased each other about how we're just creating a 'hallway' movie, where the entire film is just going through a hallway for two hours in one single direction. That was the biggest charm of this film, but also at the same time a very scary handicap. I had very complex feelings about it, although I did try to see it as just a cinematic challenge.

"I think a lot of the energy in the film comes from that setup; the fact that it all takes place in this very narrow, linear, and long space. I think that the film's energy really depends on that setup because there are no detours that these characters can take: you have those who are trying to move forward in Curtis and the rebels who are fighting for a revolution... their singular goal is to just tread forward, but you have the soldiers holding onto the axes trying to stop them, and none of these people can go the other way—all they can do is clash."

THIS SPREAD "Sometimes it's cheaper to build the whole set because you have 150 or 200 shots in it and each one of those would be a VFX shot, so it would be more expensive to do it that way—not necessarily the best. You try to build as much as possible."—Eric Durst

"WE'RE JUST CREATING A 'HALLWAY' MOVIE, WHERE THE ENTIRE FILM IS JUST GOING THROUGH A HALLWAY FOR TWO HOURS IN ONE SINGLE DIRECTION. THAT WAS THE BIGGEST CHARM OF THIS FILM, BUT ALSO AT THE SAME TIME A VERY SCARY HANDICAP."

BONG JOON HO

PIECE BY PIECE:
TAIL SECTION

"Endless freight cars, dark and filthy, like alleys in a poor village. Tail-section passengers, shabbily dressed, looking like vagrants, stand in cramped, packed rows of five across... row after row, further and further into the next car, like a cave..."

This is the screenplay description of the tail section. The passengers are clustered shoulder to shoulder like cattle and the camera is right in there with them. It was important for the filmmakers that the viewer felt as constricted and uncomfortable as the characters on-screen, so they designed the sets with that in mind.

"I didn't like the idea of taking the sides off the car sets and limiting ourselves to the left and right tracking shots," says stunt coordinator Julian Spencer. "I said to Director Bong, 'During that fight, if it's going to last a minute long, you'll really have some very physically tired men, and you'll think you're with them... Chris Evans would trip, he would stumble, he

would fall over, and I said to him this was what I wanted, be prepared for it, because that stuff happens in a real fight, and especially in a small working area like that train. Even though it was a big wide train on a stage, when you get twenty or thirty guys in there, it suddenly becomes very small."

To build the sets, the filmmakers called on the local craftsman, whose experience showed Dooho Choi that they had made the right choice in basing themselves out of Prague. "It turned out to be the best possible decision because, if you've ever been to Prague, the first thing you notice is the incredible architecture. The conventional wisdom is to bring department heads in from the US/UK, but in this case, having a local production designer managing the art department turned out to be critical. Ondřej [Nekvasil] had strong relationships with Barrandov, the construction crews, the SFX company that designed and built the gimbal, and all the other sub-departments, so it was all seamless and efficient."

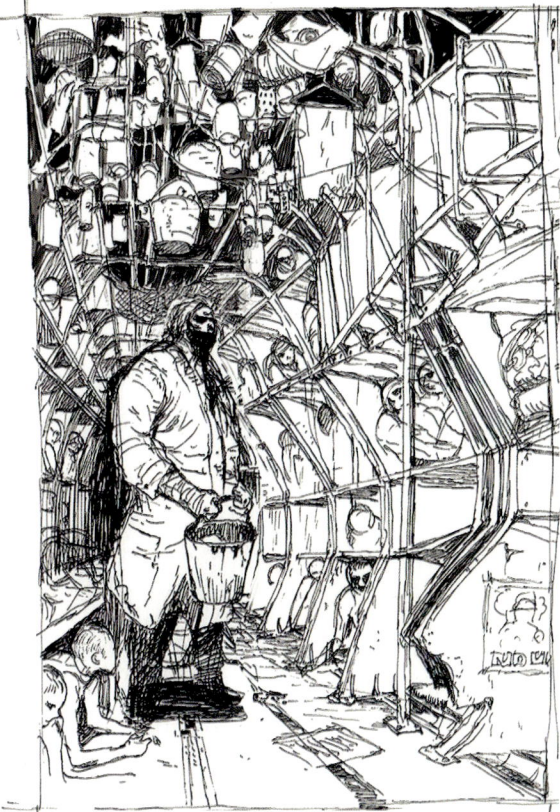

THIS SPREAD Concept artwork of the tail section and its inhabitants. In this art, the area looks more than ever like a refugee or prisoner-of-war camp—a freezing, ramshackle stalag. The details in these pieces show the level to which this world has been discussed: people crammed in next to water tanks and sleeping in spare bathtubs.

THIS SPREAD There are people with haunted, hollow-eyed faces everywhere in the tail section art, with the black and white pieces bringing to mind the hopeless souls in Gustave Doré's illustrations for *The Divine Comedy*.
OPPOSITE BOTTOM RIGHT Photo from the dressed tail section set, featuring an image from the original *Snowpiercer* graphic novel—an image that would act as a frontispiece for the reissued English-language collections from Titan Comics.

There was a unified vision amongst the crew, with each department working together to create this area of physical and psychological degradation that will birth a revolution.

"Color is hugely important," emphasizes hair and makeup designer Jeremy Woodhead. "The rear of the train had to look different from the front. This is shown not just in makeup, but in costumes and sets. I worked closely with Catherine George the costume designer and adopted her palette for each character. All the rear-of-the-train characters were dirty, brown, and grey with flashes of stained color, while the front-of-train characters were above all else clean, but also neat, polished, and brighter colors."

This is echoed by Catherine George, "We thought a lot about what would have been left over from their escape... the smell, the cold, and what they could piece together from what was around... We talked a lot with production designer Ondřej Nekvasil, who's a genius, and the set design was pieced together with things that were left over."

Ridley Scott's 1979 classic *Alien* is famous for not only its creature but its set design, with a futuristic world that in no way feels futuristic but is instead messy, tangible, and worn. The environments would seem to be an influence on *Snowpiercer*, but Director Bong draws a different parallel. "With *Alien* and *Snowpiercer*, the basic setup and storyline are very different. In the first *Alien* film, a lot of people praised the great creature design and Ridley Scott's visual sensibility, but surprisingly, what a lot of people don't talk about is the incredible ensemble of that cast. You have the characters split into blue-collar and white-collar, and you really feel the vivid conversations between the working-class characters. A lot of actors in the film—such as Sigourney Weaver and John Hurt—actually came from theater, they're stage actors. The film really felt like a story of the working class, although it is set in this spaceship, and that was something that was very memorable to me. I don't know if it was a direct influence on *Snowpiercer*, but it is something that comes into my mind."

THIS SPREAD "For me, it was like a new type of *Brazil* (1985)—the [Terry] Gilliam movie. A strange society, very strange humor together with very powerful scenes. Very bizarre characters, some of them could be funny but some are really dangerous, and some moments twist in a way you're not expecting." —Ondřej Nekvasil
OPPOSITE TOP Concept art showing a different version of the interior of the tail section, more orderly and evenly designed for habitation—still a far cry from the areas nearer the front occupied by the more affluent.

"WITH CLAUDE IN THE YELLOW SUIT—WITH THE TRAIN—THERE'S A CERTAIN TONE AND COLOR TO THE TAIL SECTION, AND WE WANTED HER TO 'POP' WHEN SHE CAME. SO WE TESTED A LOT OF YELLOW COLORS AND THAT ONE SEEMED BEST. THE SAME WITH THE MILITARY UNIFORMS, THAT BLUE COLOR THAT WE USED. WE DID A LOT OF COLOR-TESTING."

CATHERINE GEORGE

"THE REAR TRAIN PASSENGERS WERE ALL GIVEN A WASH OF DIRT THAT SUGGESTED THEY HAD NO WASHING FACILITIES AND THAT THE DIRT WAS CHRONIC AND PORE DEEP. DIRECTOR BONG WAS VERY INSISTENT THAT THE DIRT SHOULD LOOK LIKE IT WENT BACK YEARS AND WAS NOT SUPERFICIAL RECENT DIRT. SO I DEVELOPED A TECHNIQUE OF FLOATING ON BLACK DIRT WITH LARGE MOP BRUSHES LIKE A WATERCOLOR THAT WOULD SINK INTO THE PORES, AND WHEN BUILT UP IN LAYERS, GAVE US THE YEARS OF OLD GRIME THAT WE WERE LOOKING FOR."

JEREMY WOODHEAD

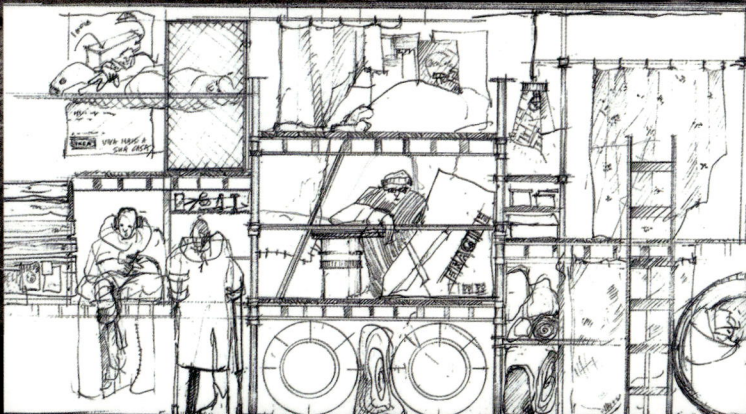

"EVERY SINGLE THING YOU SEE IS A TANGIBLE ENVIRONMENT THAT YOU CAN PLAY OFF. THE DETAIL IS JUST SO PHENOMENAL. THE DIRT WAS DIRT. THE GRIME WAS GRIME. IT ACTUALLY FELT LIKE YOU WERE ON THIS TRAIN. IT FELT LIKE THIS TRAIN HAD BEEN RUNNING FOR YEARS AND YOU WERE A SECOND-CLASS CITIZEN."

CHRIS EVANS

For his own incredible ensemble, the sets being created at Barrandov Studios were like nothing they had seen before. Chris Evans—no stranger to big budgets and state-of-the-art film tech—describes the first time he laid eyes on the train. "I really remember the first couple of days because so much of it was predicated on this intangible understanding of what it will look like. I remember the first days that I was able to go to see the set. You arrive in Prague and you have sittings and you have rehearsals, and one day they said, 'Would you like to come down and actually see some sections of the train?' and I just said, 'Oh my God!' I've never had a set piece be so informative to a character, ever. EVER. I've done movies where, for instance, your office set tells you a little bit about the work you do, the home tells you a little bit about the life you've made for yourself. But this train is a character. This is *so* informative to everything about who Curtis is, so to go to the set and actually walk through each of the separate cars of the train... At the end of the day, I just asked if it was okay if I stayed there for a few hours. Can my driver just pick me up again in three or four hours? I'd love just to sit in here alone for a little while, and they very graciously let me do it. I just kind of went from car to car. I just sat in the space for a while. One of the fun things about acting in general is we're just big kids playing make believe. You got so much information from this train. It was really fun, despite being a dark-edged space and a dire environment, it was really enjoyable to just be alone in that train for a while and imagine what it would be like to be in that circumstance."

THIS SPREAD "Something I remember in particular is just the smell, especially when we shot all the tail-section scenes. You had hundreds of extras in the train set... the entire set would be filled with carbon dioxide, the air would be so stale, and it's very hot inside the set because of all the lighting, people would be sweating... a lot of the extras came without taking a shower to make the whole thing look more realistic, so by the afternoon, things would become smelly." —Bong Joon Ho
OPPOSITE BOTTOM RIGHT Clark Middleton, who plays the Painter, flanked by artist Jean-Marc Rochette and writer Benjamin Legrand.

PIECE BY PIECE:
QUARANTINE, PRISON
& GUARD SECTIONS

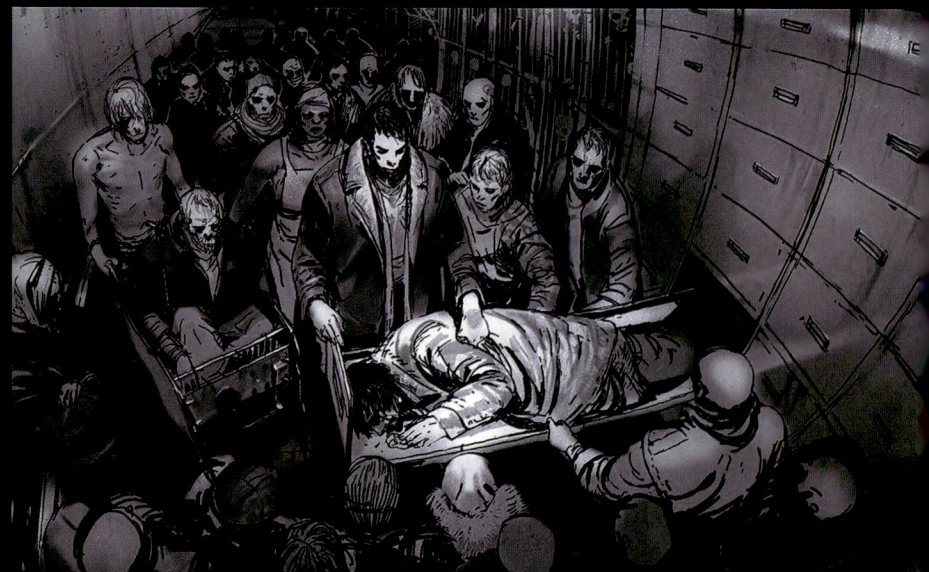

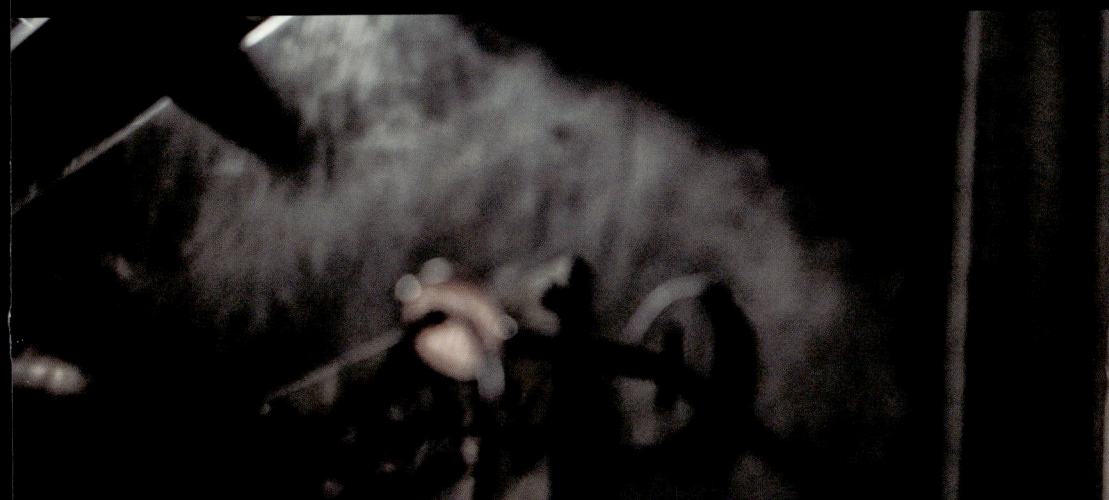

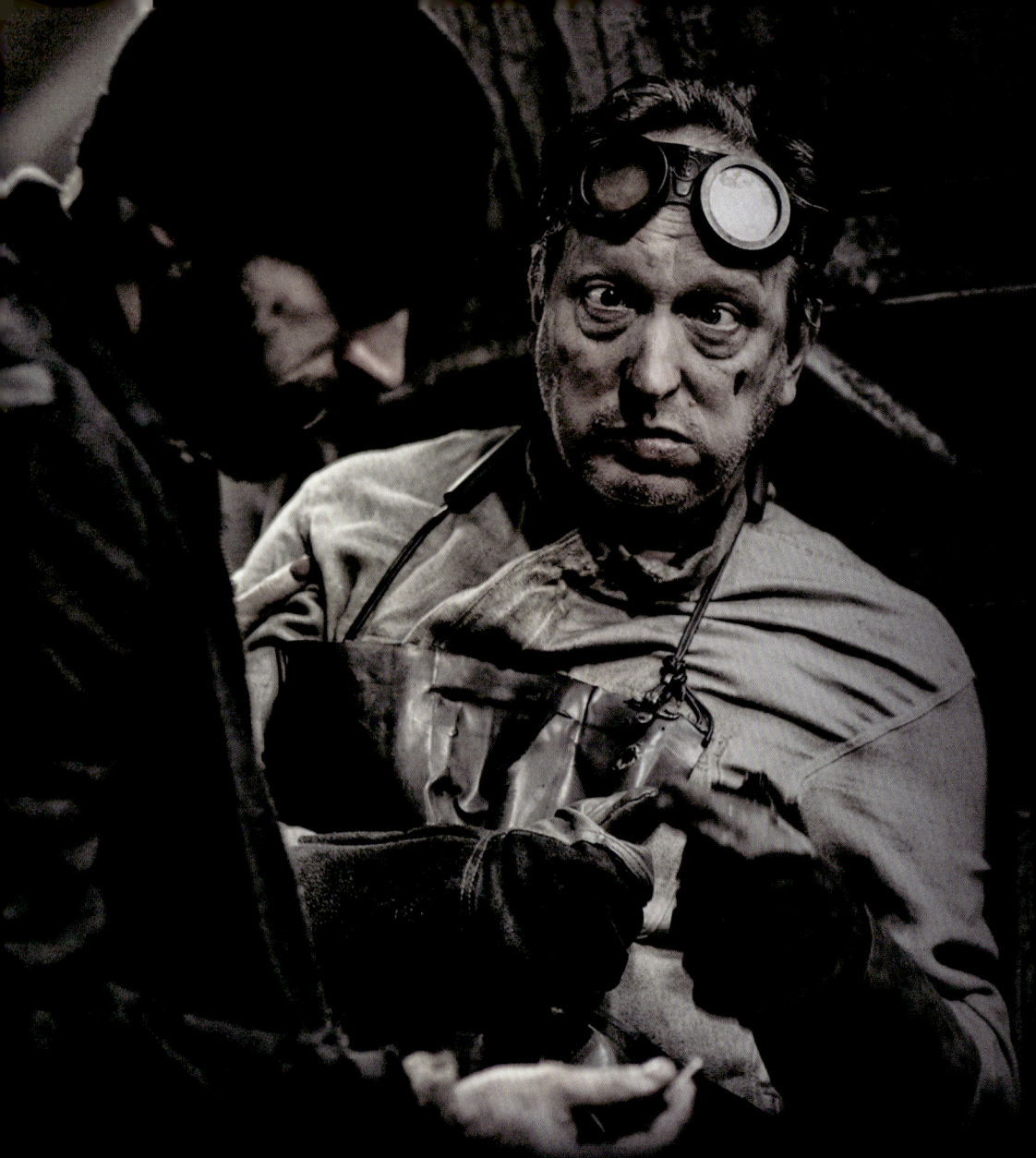

PIECE BY PIECE:

PROTEIN BLOCK SECTION

"AS SOON AS HE GOT ON SET I RECOGNIZED PAUL LAZAR FROM *THE SILENCE OF THE LAMBS* [1991], WHICH IS ONE OF MY FAVORITE FILMS OF ALL TIME, AND I COULDN'T BELIEVE I'M IN A MOVIE WITH THIS GUY!"

JAMIE BELL

THIS SPREAD "Sometimes with films like *Snowpiercer*, it's not unheard of to have a lot of CGI stuff. You have maybe within your immediate three or four feet a tangible set but then the backdrop and the expanse of your surrounding area is all CGI. But these trains—you're inside the train, you are in this train." —Chris Evans

PIECE BY PIECE:
ABANDONED
SECTION

PIECE BY PIECE:

WATER SUPPLY SECTION

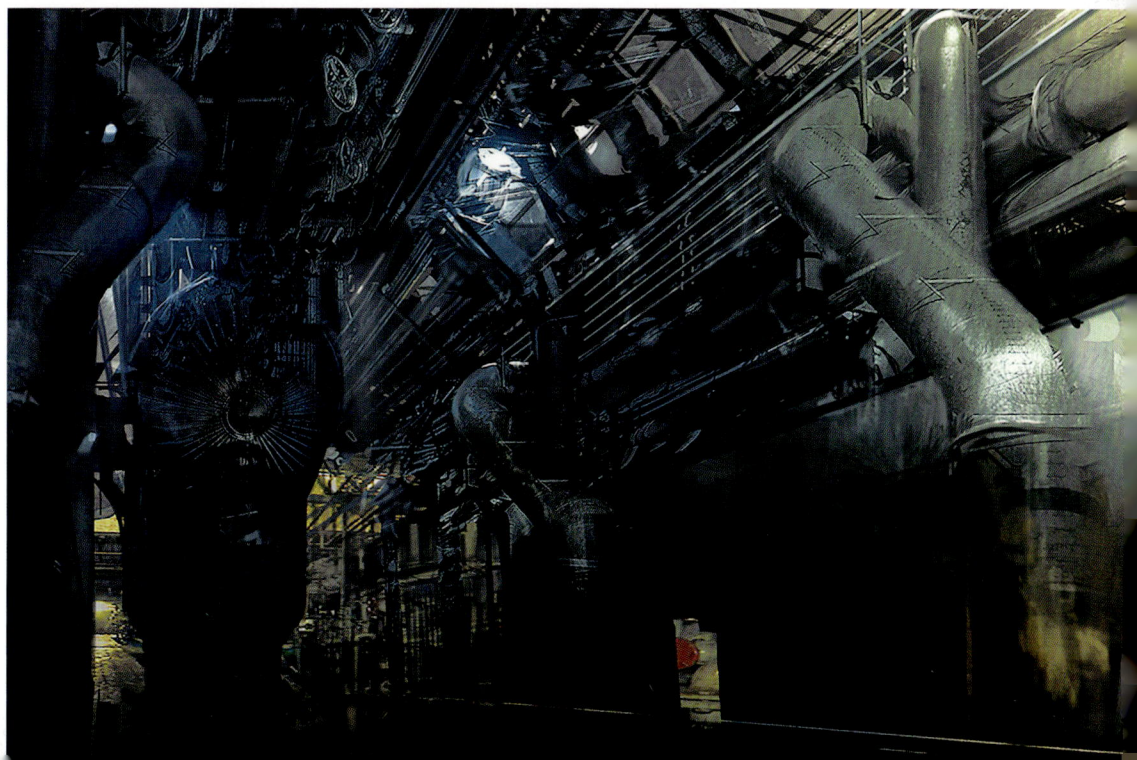

OPPOSITE PAGE Some imagery in *Snowpiercer* is as close as Bong Joon Ho has come to making a horror film, not only in terms of gore and violence but couching the violence and actions of others in a way that speaks to a deep darkness in humanity. Concept art such as this is post-apocalyptic and almost nihilistic.

THIS PAGE "It looked like people had been there for a long time, building all these sets. I realized, wow, this thing is really happening." —Eric Durst

PIECE BY PIECE:

GREENHOUSE

Seeing, feeling, and smelling trees and flowers should be perfectly natural, but for the tail sectioners—especially those born on the train—entering the greenhouse car is like stepping onto an alien planet. For someone like Yona, who knows only the metal train and the endless winter outside, it has to be explained to her what soil is. It is an entirely new sensory and visual experience.

ABOVE AND OPPOSITE BOTTOM Comparison of concept art versus final film setup, showing how closely and carefully Director Bong plans in advance. **OPPOSITE TOP LEFT** For Tanya and the other tail sectioners, fresh fruit is almost miraculous.

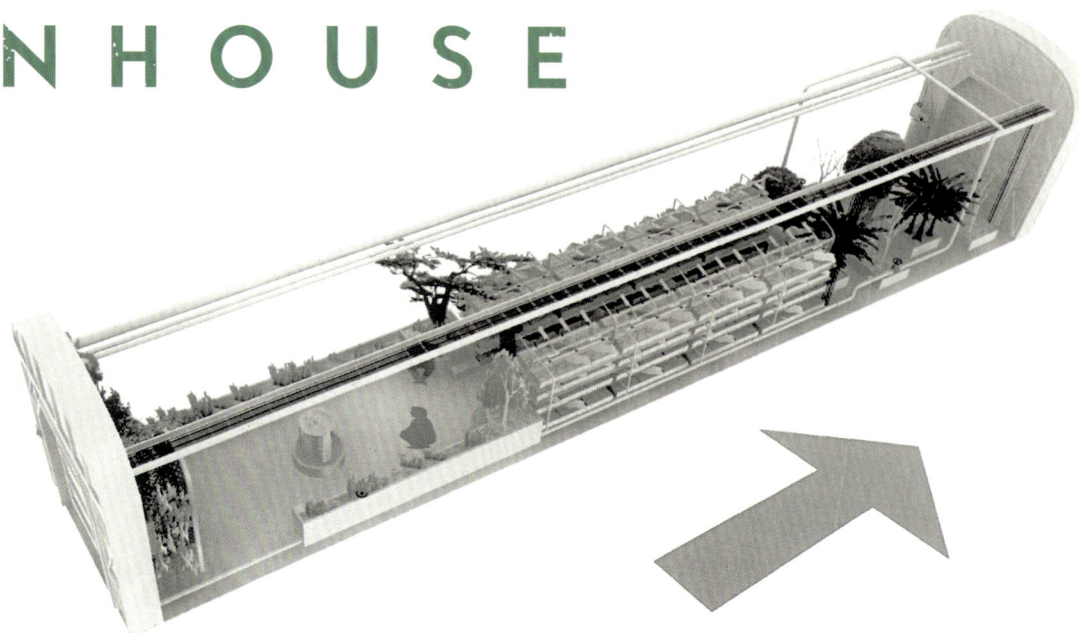

Ondřej Nekvasil explains how they created this sudden influx of life and color. "Regarding the color palette in the tail section, without the light, [it was] really dark, so we were using dark grey colors and metal colors. After, we went to some technical sections and we were using a lot of colors like aluminum and metal, that type of thing. But there was still nothing full of color. That was the reason that once we'd passed through the technical sections into the first class, the first moment they were stepping into the greenhouse—a really nice greenhouse with a lot of trees and a little fountain, plants with tomatoes or whatever—we were thinking it has to be a really big jump, so we were not using some of these colors in the back section. We didn't use that green at all, we didn't use blue. That was the way we were trying to create a really big jump there."

LEFT Concept art showing Curtis, Namgoong, and a much younger Yona. The art also shows a camera angle not in keeping with the directional rules established by Director Bong and his director of photography, Hong Kyung Pyo.
BELOW Bong Joon Ho, Tilda Swinton, Ewen Bremner, and Octavia Spencer talk through the scene on the greenhouse set.

PIECE BY PIECE:
AQUARIUM

In the story, they break from the industrial wasteland of the tail section and fight their way into a new section of the train, one unlike anything the train babies have seen before. There are some brief moments of calm and unexpected beauty as Mason leads the survivors through the greenhouse and into the aquarium. Suddenly, the color palette of the movie changes again as we enter a world of blues, with flashes of tropical marine life as the fish swim through the clear water. Forever inventive with the geography of the train sets, the production designer, the director of photography, and Director Bong created a car where the aquarium is in the walls and ceilings, and the characters walk through a glass tunnel. Because of what it would have taken to create an actual aquarium on set, complete with live specimens, the production turned to the VFX department to create something realistic to add in during postproduction.

"THE MOST VIRTUAL CAR IN THE WHOLE FILM WAS THE AQUARIUM."

ERIC DURST

"Everything that was outside the train was a CG environment," explains Ondřej Nekvasil. "Everything inside was 90% a real 360 set. Only difference was the aquarium, which was a CG aquarium. That was a really big discussion at the beginning. We put the numbers together and we realized that building an aquarium was so expensive. We knew the guys that could give us the glass and all of that, we were able to provide it, but technically there was the money question: what was the cost of the CG aquarium compared to the cost of the physical aquarium? That sushi bar was a real place, but the rest was green [screen]. The aquarium was the CG set. We had a plan to build it but realized it was too expensive for such a short scene. When they put these numbers together, building the real stuff was more expensive than CG. They built a whole environment."

For this environment, Eric Durst used one of the five VFX houses employed on the movie, Method, who would go on to work with Bong Joon Ho again on the titular character of *Okja* (2017).

"The most virtual car in the whole film was the aquarium," confirms Durst. "We had some water reflectors, so you get a 'caustic' light effect that happens. Alex the director of photography had some

OPPOSITE A pencil sketch and finished concept art of the aquarium.
TOP CENTER AND RIGHT The actors working against green screens for computer graphics that would be added in much later.

pretty inventive ways of doing it. We had a skeleton of the aquarium, just the shape of it so everyone could get the feel of it, but I'm really happy about how that worked out. [There was] a lot of research on the fish and how it looked. There's an aquarium that's very similar to that one—a glass tunnel that you go through—so we used that as inspiration. We made the creatures up and used reference material. I think the aquarium tunnel was in Vancouver. Mark Brakespear, who was the VFX supervisor at Method, did a huge amount on that and really was a great supervisor in providing that."

In this moment of relative tranquillity, Mason leads Curtis and the others to the sushi bar for a discussion about balance and the merits of fresh fish versus protein bars. As they talk, there is some barely discernible background music playing. While it may be a minor note, it nonetheless called for the film's composer, Marco Beltrami, to create something suitable for the mood of the environment—and which ended up being unexpectedly challenging.

"There was one little scene that was super hard for me," Beltrami recalls. "It took forever to crack it. It was a very benign little scene when they're in the sushi car. Bong had wanted this ambient music almost to be playing in the sushi car. At first, I thought maybe it's the music of the outside because we'd been talking about that, but Bong said, 'No, I want it to be like a *Deer Hunter* [1978] moment.' I couldn't figure out what that meant. '*Deer Hunter*' moment? So he says more of like a classical piece. So I wrote something reminiscent of a Chopin piece. That was the one scene that was really hard to crack for whatever reason. It seemed very simple, but I think I must have rewritten that seven or eight times. The rest of it was good."

THIS PAGE Even the fittings, the background, underneath, and the very structure of the car needed to be dressed for green screen to fit with how the aquarium would be inserted digitally.

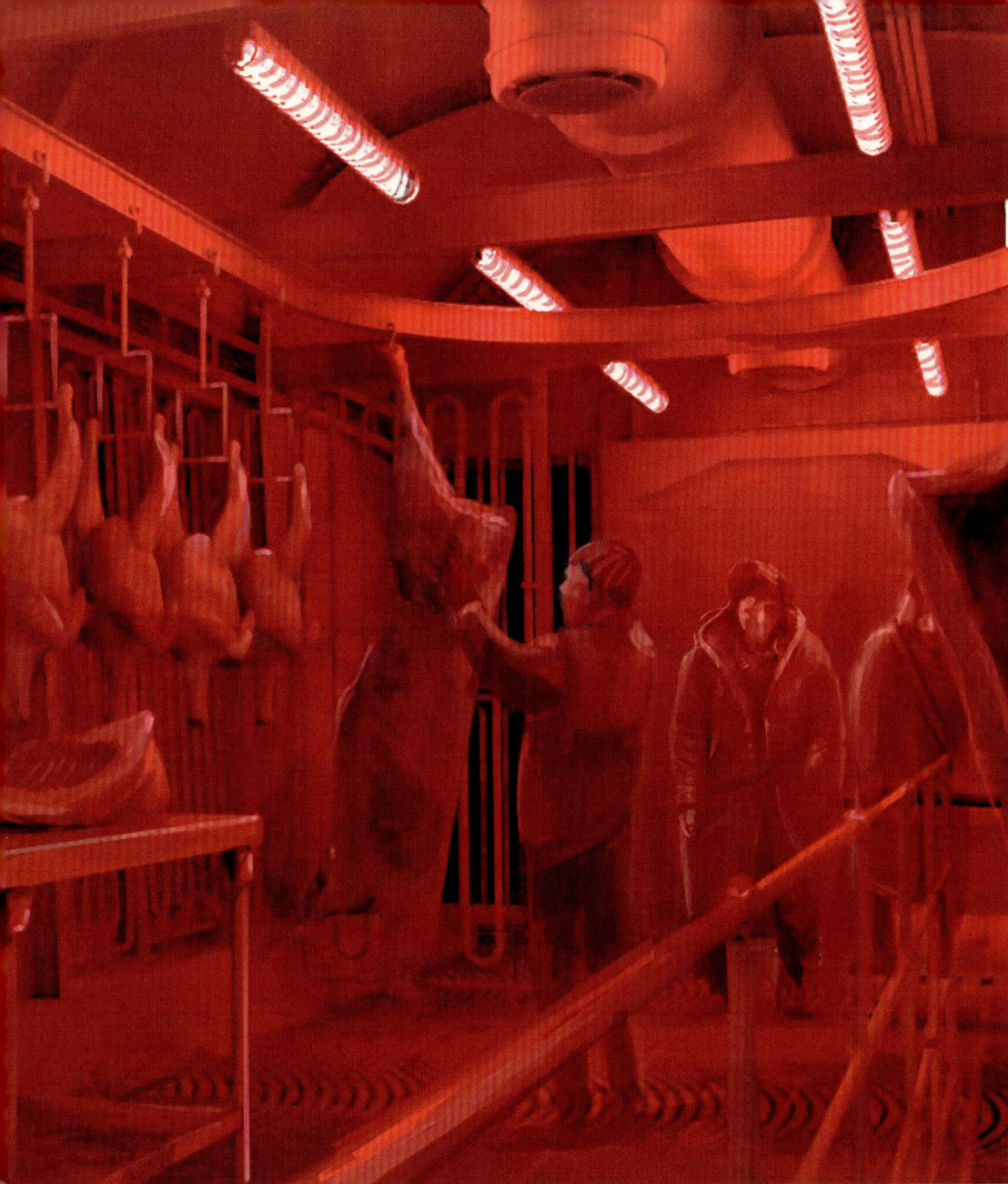

PIECE BY PIECE:
ABATTOIR

THIS PAGE The abattoir: a setting Bong Joon Ho would return to with even more bloody and vivid effect in his 2017 movie, *Okja*.
RIGHT "My department was a decent size... We decided at the beginning that each [of the] set designers would do one car, so we all had a few cars in different sections." —Ondřej Nekvasil

CLASSROOM

Religion has not played an especially prevalent part in Bong Joon Ho's filmography so far. From crime dramas to environmentally infused adventures, he has concentrated on people, the decisions they make, and the consequences of their actions. Monsters may climb out of the Han River, but it stampedes across a world we know.

Karl Marx famously said that, "Religion is the opium of the people,"

and if the train houses all aspects of society within it, it is only right that religion is also present. Where power and privilege are so important, it is essential that order, balance, and the status quo are maintained, and this is where religion plays a part. The continuation of Snowpiercer and its values must be assured, so there is no better time to enforce these values than at an early age.

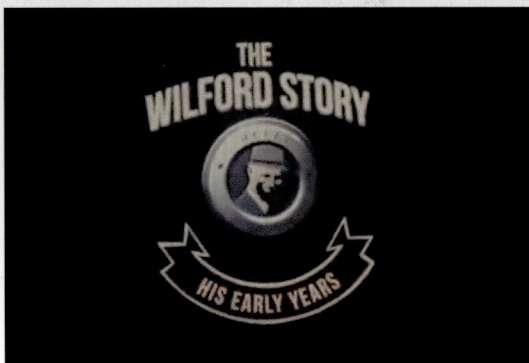

THIS SPREAD The classroom and the 'Frozen Seven.'
BELOW "Bong did every single detail, every single shot by himself and he was really not happy that he couldn't shoot part of the documentary because he had to be on set and, because of the schedule, we were shooting [it at the same time as the main unit]. But he had an online connection and he was commanding everything we shot in that castle. It's just a few shots in that documentary movie about Wilford, which is shown in the school sequence." —Ondřej Nekvasil

"I think [the religious aspects in the film] come from people worshipping the engine and its creator Wilford especially," says Director Bong, "and in the classroom car, you have the children singing this hymn about the engine and Wilford. In the original graphic novel, in part two, you actually do have a priest character who performs a religious ceremony. In the film, it's not that obvious, of course, and I think it comes from the basic setup of treating the engine as God, and the religious leaders of this cult of the engine are Mason and Wilford.

"This may be more important, but not only do they worship the engine, but their sense of religion also instils a fear of escaping the train and going outside. I think one of the roles of religion is actually to instil fear. You have mantras like, *You will be punished if you covet your neighbor's wife*, things like that. In the film, you have the 'Frozen Seven,' where these children are shown the seven people who froze to death outside, and they are taught to have fear of the outside world. It is quite a cruel way to educate children, but in that sense, you also see how religion functions in this story and the classroom sequence."

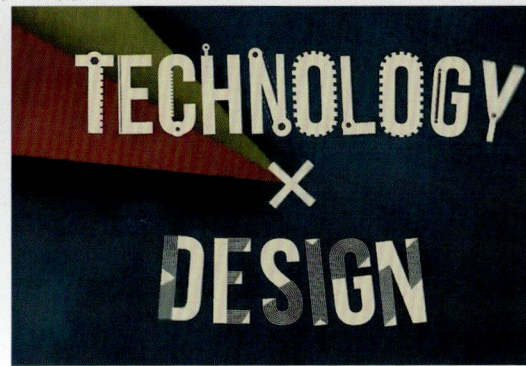

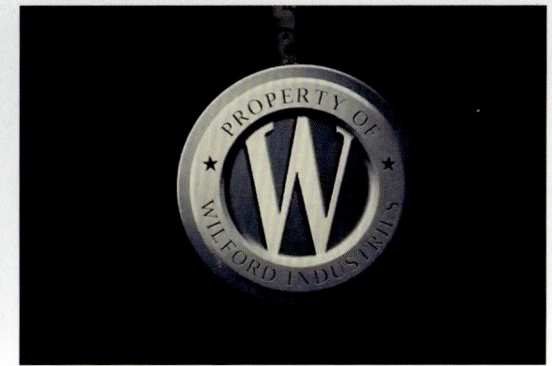

"WE HAD A DIFFERENT CONCEPT...
A VERY COOL CLASSROOM, WHERE
EVERYBODY HAS A UNIFORM. THAT
WAS A DIFFERENT OPTION, BUT
WE REALIZED THAT WE WOULD
GO WITH THE CRAZINESS. IT'S SO
OPTIMISTIC THAT IT'S SCARY."

ONDŘEJ NEKVASIL

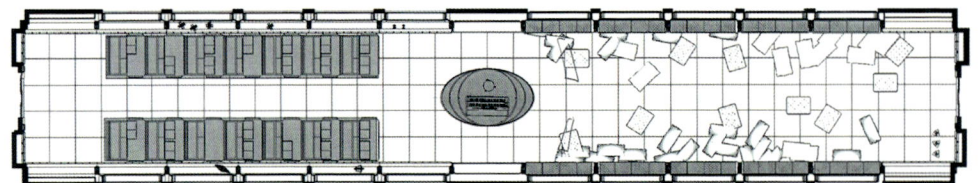

The classroom scene is one of the most entertaining and yet also one of the most unsettling sections of the film. With the first half of the film building up such furious momentum about getting to the front and fighting to get there, upon finding themselves in the classroom, our protagonists learn there is something stranger going on aboard this train. There are more obstacles to fixing this system than men with axes.

This deeply disturbing and darkly satirical scene was created with bright colors and with a production decision and attitude that contrasts the damning politics. Ondřej Nekvasil explains, "We used a very drastic color palette in the classroom, which was really important to us. The teacher is so friendly and so nice that you have goosebumps just hearing her. She's like a little Nazi or little Communist. We said we have to make that classroom so colorful that you don't want to be there. We didn't want to go with just the normal colorful classroom, with nice walls and colorful details. We said let's make something completely crazy that it will be a classroom but it's weird. These colors are too bright and too strange. We asked some kids in the schools to make some props for us out of paper, and paint some pictures for us as well. We wanted that to be our craziest moment. The twist that happens in the classroom was enormous, so we thought it would be good to have a classroom that is not oppressive but it's so optimistic that it's oppressive."

The visual impact of the sequence is so jarring and fits so perfectly with this dystopia, but it almost went in another direction, one that symbolized an alternative take on a class-defined world and a repressive rather than oppressive society.

"We had a different concept," confirms Nekvasil. "We were keen on the idea of the classroom being like Victorian England. A very cool classroom, where everybody has a uniform. That was a different option, but we realized that we would go with the craziness. It's so optimistic that it's scary."

OPPOSITE PAGE Different scenarios for the classroom set, gradually bringing in more color until eventually reaching the eye-popping colors of the final depiction. THIS PAGE Shooting Alison Pill's short but impactful character arc from perky teacher and enthusiastic choirmistress to cold-blooded killer.

PIECE BY PIECE:
LIVING QUARTERS

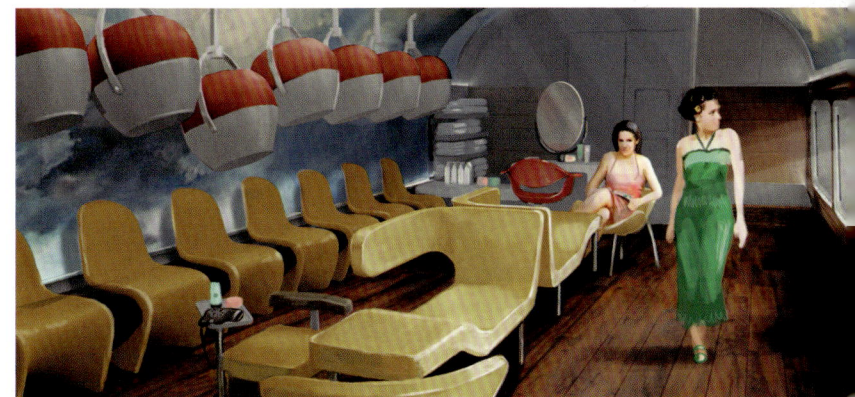

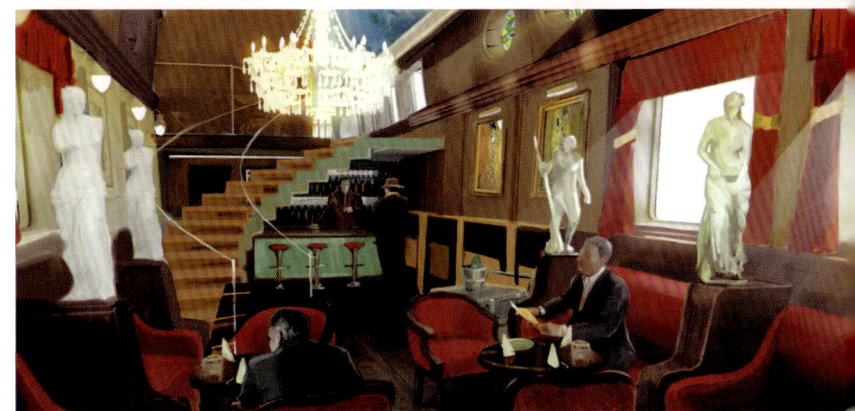

THIS SPREAD Concept art versus set photo showing a grand lounge area, where indulgence and affectation is valued more than commonality and togetherness. The *mise-en-scène*, showing the change in set design, character design and the story's arc, is clearly communicated and coded in each set. The heavily furnished interiors—with matching passengers— is in keeping with the great 'train films' in cinema from *The Lady Vanishes* (1938) to *Murder on the Orient Express* (1974).

PIECE BY PIECE:
SWIMMING POOL

The classroom—which in a normal world would be a safe space—sees more violence and death. Their numbers slimming, Curtis and his fellow freedom fighters move through a handful of different train cars, each more plush than the last. They go past a tailor's—which feels as exclusive and high quality as anything on Savile Row—dentist rooms, a hair salon, and a cocktail bar. In none of these places do the other passengers pay any attention to these tail sectioners; perhaps they are too involved in their easy bourgeoisie existence or perhaps they don't even recognize these filthy, malnourished people as being of the same race as them. It throws into stark relief the very ideal of revolution if it goes unnoticed by those being revolted against.

They then find themselves in the swimming pool car. This car offers new visuals and compositions for the audience to adjust to, featuring a flatter, more open space that creates the illusion of width among the other cars that feel longer and thinner. This was a very deliberate decision, but nothing was done for the sake of it: the how and the why of any car had to be discussed far in advance.

"We had different ideas for each car and some cars were really strange," recalls Nekvasil. "Like a whole car was a swimming pool and you have to walk across it to cross the next car... It was in the pre-prep period that we were really able to discuss all this stuff and resolve most of the issues. We had some discussions about the gimbals—where would it be, how difficult would it be to have a gimbal and a swimming pool, are we doing that or not? Are we doing a swimming pool with a glass wall or are we having solid walls? All that was discussed at the beginning and doing so was the key for how we were able to pull it off successfully."

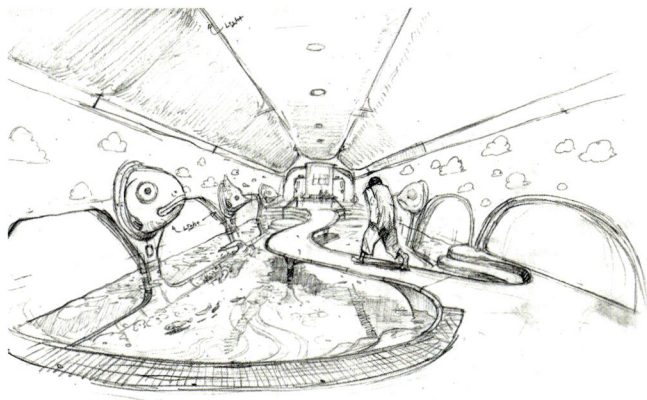

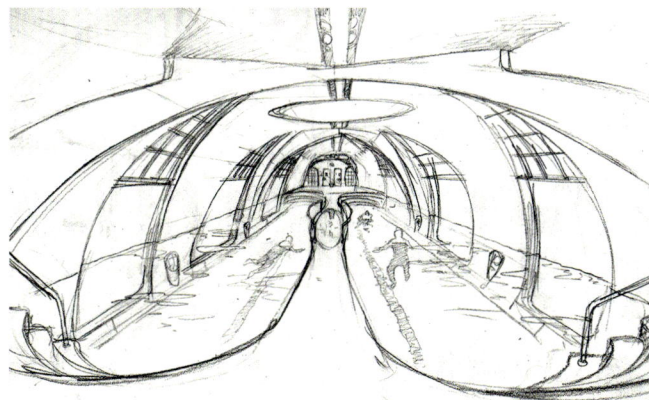

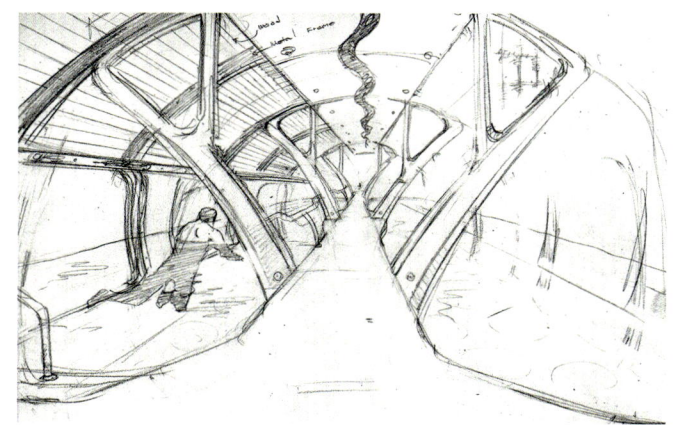

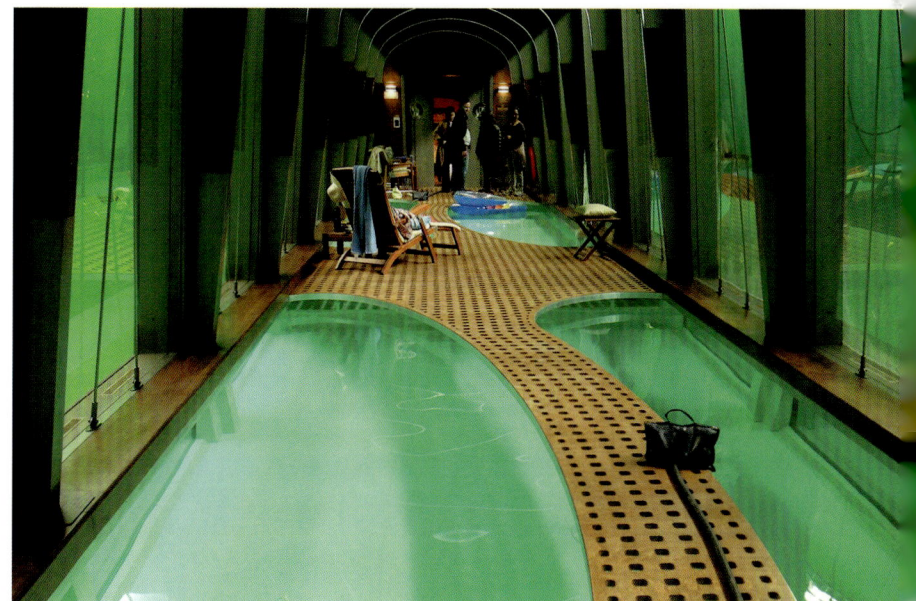

THIS SPREAD "The sketches were really important and part of the process. They show how we were thinking about the cars, how the train is moving and all of that. They were great and [it was] unusual to get such information from a director so early." —Ondřej Nekvasil

The Snowpiercer moves into a big bend and suddenly a bullet hits the glass. Franco the Elder is in pursuit and is firing at them from a previous car. In many films, an action scene exists purely for excitement and needs no explanation, but the *Snowpiercer* team were not satisfied with that. The geography of this scene, the reason for it, had to make sense, even if its justification is something that the audience would never even think about.

"The reason why the swimming pool car has big glass windows and is open and distinctive," explains Nekvasil, "was because of that curve, the big turn, and suddenly the guys who are following them can see them and shoot through the curve. It was really important to have the design, so you can see them and they are very significant and visible within the car... We discussed how to make the very fact of the train doing this turn more believable. We decided there was an abandoned mining city with these buildings and all these technical structures in the curve. That the train is doing a curve in the middle of nowhere because there is some sort of city in the turn and you would have stopped in a train station once."

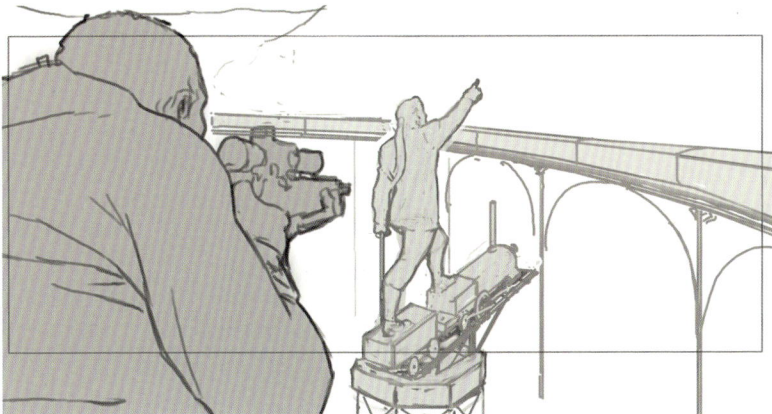

THIS SPREAD Planning and executing one of the most complicated sequences in the movie, as Curtis and Franco the Elder conduct a gunfight directly at one another, despite being in different carriages. The heavily windowed area needed to be completely CGI beyond the glass.

PIECE BY PIECE:
SAUNA

After the open, cool space of the swimming pool, Curtis, Tanya, Namgoong, Yona, and Grey find themselves in the tight, sweaty sauna section. They are under attack from Franco the Elder and seemingly have nowhere left to run. It sees the sad and grisly end of Tanya and Grey. The scene is played without music and is intimate and inescapable. The demise of these characters is hard to face, not because of the violence, but because of the emotions.

"Director Bong's films can appear more violent than they really are," says Dooho Choi. "When you look at the shots and what's being shown, you'll see an axe swing, but you don't actually see it hit the person. In very few instances do you see contact. You hear the sound and see the reaction, the blood-splatter, but you don't actually see an axe cut off a limb. He's not all that interested in gore. It's just a combination of what's going on in the scene and the tension that has been building. It makes the audience feel there's more going on than they're actually seeing."

The centerpiece axe fight has moments of slow motion, elements of horror-thriller almost with the night vision, and the stylized, impressionistic arrival of the torches. But the sauna confrontation is more matter of fact and reiterates the philosophy of Wilford and his cronies: that life is disposable. This is especially true with the death of Tanya, who we have been hoping to see reunited with her son.

"I'm quite passionate about showing what damage a gun can do to people," says Julian Spencer. "Being in the military, I've seen what bullets can do, and I hate the Hollywood style. A bullet makes a small hole going in and a massive hole coming out, and people don't fly back six feet when they get hit. People don't always scream initially when the pain gets bad, so I just tried to make it as realistic as I could with that one. If you get hit with a bullet, you don't fly off, you just slump where you are. That's what we did on *Saving Private Ryan* (1998): you're just like a puppet with the strings cut. Bang, down, that's it—life's over."

THIS SPREAD Haunting concept art of the sauna scene, showing the closer we get to 'society's elite,' the more garish and grotesque the people become. The whole sequence somewhat resembles a heady fever dream, with Curtis almost running on empty in order to reach his final destination.
TOP LEFT Director Bong's own drawing showing the devastation wreaked by Franco the Elder.

PIECE BY PIECE:
CLUB

"We were able to think about the car designs separately and imagine that, for instance, there was a car that was a swimming pool and it was designed in this period of time and that was about fifteen years ago and the guy designed it this way, and there was also a car that was an aquarium and it was designed in a completely different style—they just put them together," explains Ondřej Nekvasil. "That was one of the concepts we agreed with Director Bong. We changed the style all the time. Bong said we are going to do some retro style: we have that lounge that is a bit 1970s/'80s. We were changing the designs and that was all based on the idea that some of these train cars could have been twenty years on the rails and he's just put them together because he likes them and he likes the design, and they're still there working."

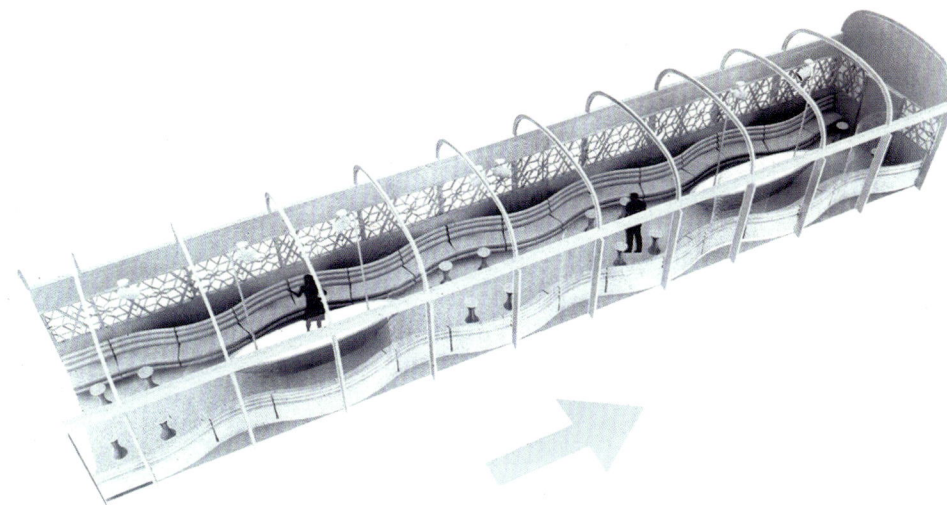

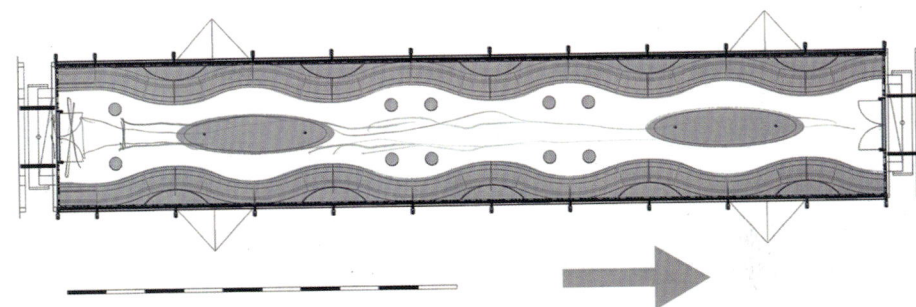

OPPOSITE A one-sighted Curtis and an alcohol-guzzling Yona seem unaware of the reveller who bears a striking resemblance to Minister Mason.
THIS PAGE Moody artwork and set plans for the club car.

PIECE BY PIECE:
OPIUM SECTION

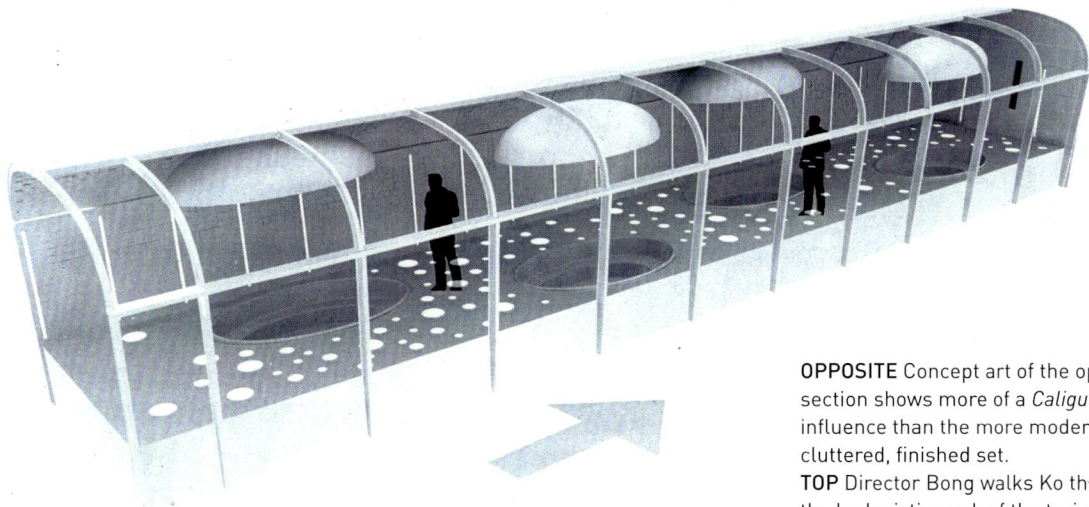

OPPOSITE Concept art of the opium section shows more of a *Caligula* (1979) influence than the more modern, cluttered, finished set.
TOP Director Bong walks Ko through the hedonistic peak of the train.

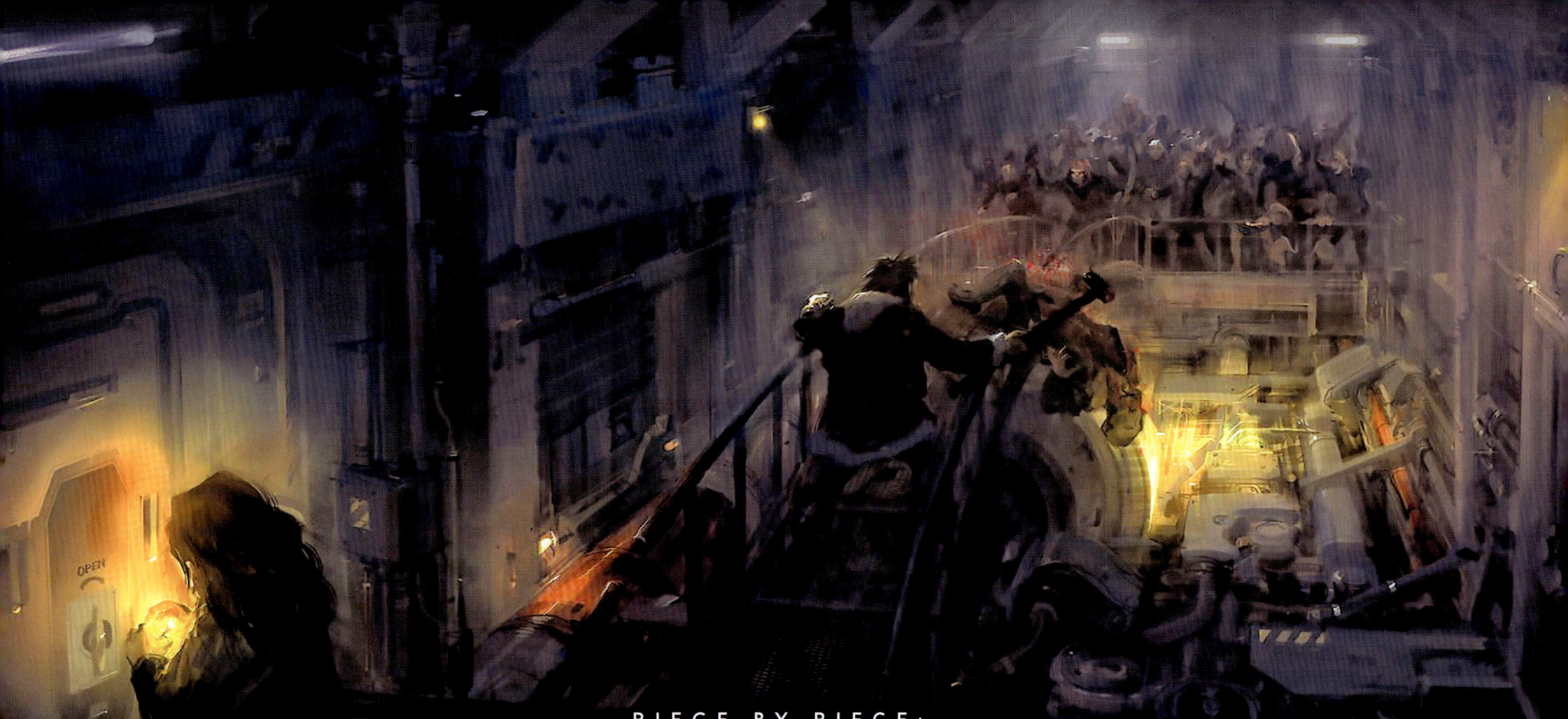

PIECE BY PIECE:
TECH & MACHINE SECTIONS

THIS SPREAD "A good portion of all the sets in the cars themselves were there. We did everything outside. We had green screen for that. The engine itself was one thing we had to build, also when they're going over that catwalk where they have that fight, with the engine parts moving and chopping one of the guys up—that was all CG as well. We tried to get as much in there as possible because of lighting and just getting that to work."—Eric Durst

"There were these strange concepts for each car," says Ondřej Nekvasil, "but technically, the idea was to do with a lot of colors in the first class. From almost like zero colors in the back, with metal colors and the grey palette up into the technical section, then after we went up to completely crazy colors in the classroom, then there's the twist, then we went slightly down, down, down, back to a colorless engine section at the end. It wasn't like you keep going up, it was more like an arch what we did with the colors."

PIECE BY PIECE:
THE SACRED ENGINE

Finally, Curtis arrives at the end of the train—or, rather, the front. By fighting, bargaining, and by sheer force of will, he is granted entry to the engine and to Wilford's lair. What he finds is not all that different to the tail section. There are no windows here and nowhere to hide. It is a confined space, and Wilford is as much a prisoner as Curtis—he just has better food.

It was important that this climactic venue either met or subverted the expectations the viewer had for it. Seeing the engine in all its glory, it has a pristine, objective, golden-ratio-style beauty to it. This tells us that the deified engine is just a machine; it is objective and purely functional. The enemy, the cause of suffering on the train, is mankind.

This is a lot to express from a design standpoint and accordingly became a major task, as Bong Joon Ho explains, "We had to design each individual train car and especially the engine section. The perpetual engine of this train is a very important element of the film. The entire train worships this engine like it is some sort of religion. We had three different conceptual artists work on the engine car and we would have weekly meetings and try hundreds of different things. That took a lot of time before we could even enter official preproduction."

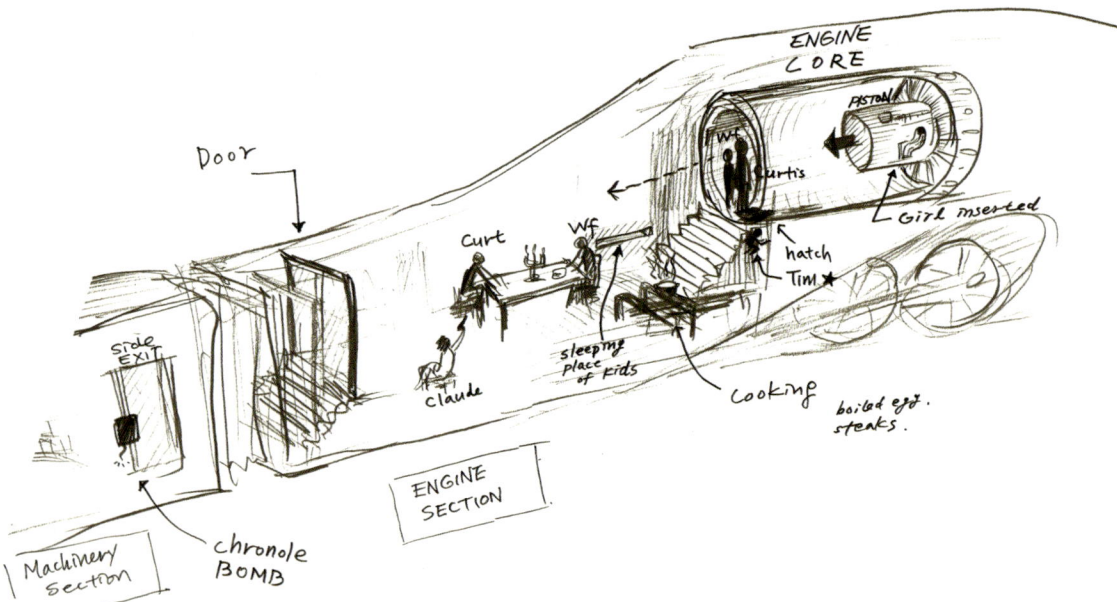

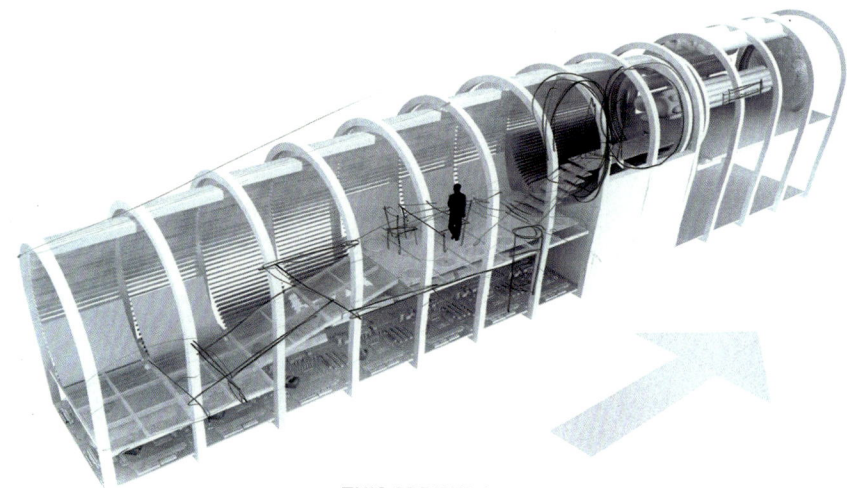

THIS SPREAD Concept art that seems influenced in part by H.R. Giger's biomechanical artwork, famously used to great effect in *Alien*.

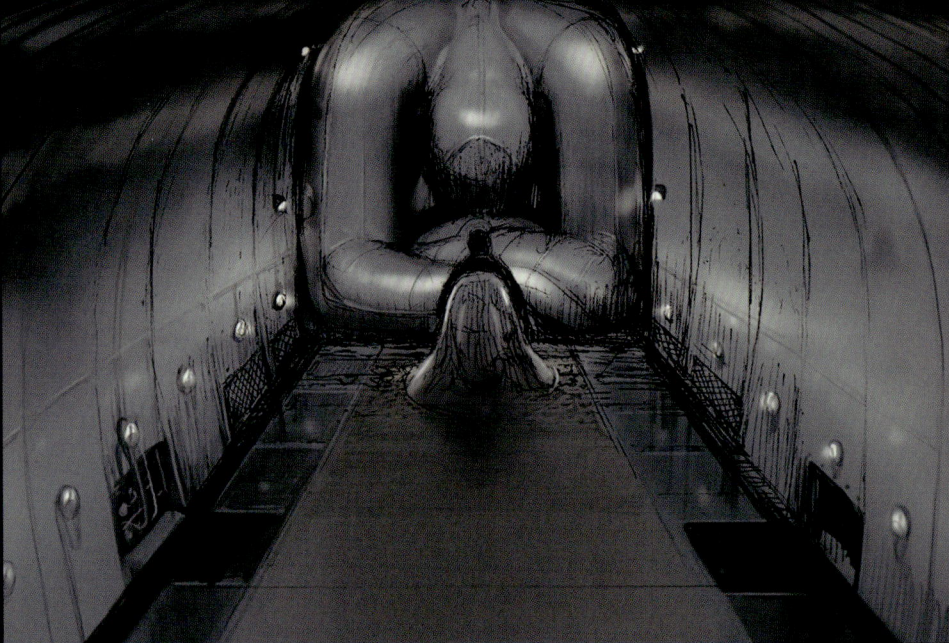

> # "THE ENTIRE TRAIN WORSHIPS THIS ENGINE LIKE IT IS SOME SORT OF RELIGION."
>
> ## BONG JOON HO

Despite being one of the 'showstopper' sets for the production, it nonetheless had to fit with the rules and motifs created throughout the whole train design. Except for two instances, the train car designs follow a horizontal rule—horizontal walls and windows constantly pulling us down the length of the train toward the engine—and the engine is no different.

"We break that horizontal line two times," says Ondřej Nekvasil. "One was that moment when they step into the greenhouse and the greenhouse was about six meters tall and suddenly they see the trees and all the greenery; and the second one was having the swimming pool and having that distinctive car seen through the large, open glass... We use that horizontal line for the engine. We had aluminium blinds, with which we created the feeling of the space and the horizontal line leading toward the engine. We worked a lot on this design, and we were looking for some details that can give us the feeling of the special moment that says *now we are inside the engine*. That was the longest process, to find the shape of the engine, and I hope that we found the right way to do it.

"It was a really tricky moment: how to show the engine? We started as a Jules Verne, Captain Nemo type of engine with a lot of pipes. We looked at spaceships—all of these types of things. Then a colleague of mine came up with the shape of the cooler, that aluminium cooler around the engine. He said, 'What if we are inside the cooler and everything that was going on was actually outside and Wilford's inside of it?' We really started thinking, *Okay, that's the right direction.*"

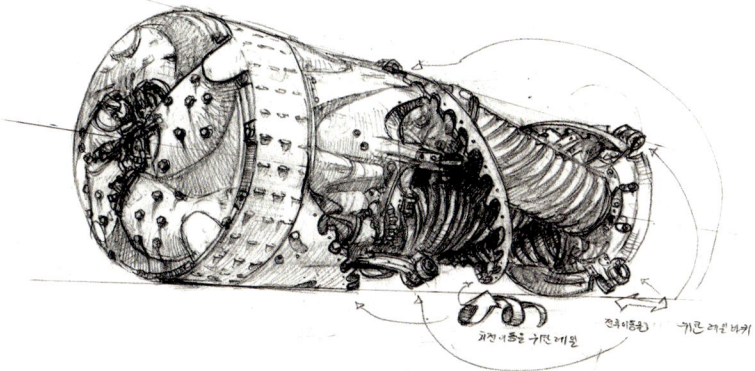

OPPOSITE TOP LEFT In this image, the engine resembles a figure bent forward in prayer, in supplication to Wilford as the god of this metal world.
THIS PAGE "I always envisioned Curtis had not necessarily been very in touch with his emotions even prior to getting on the train. I think his emotional access has only become more ossified in his time in the train, so it really was meant to be this incredibly cathartic reveal... that certainly was one of the more emotional scenes that I've ever done on a film set." —Chris Evans
RIGHT Ed Harris and Dooho Choi on set.

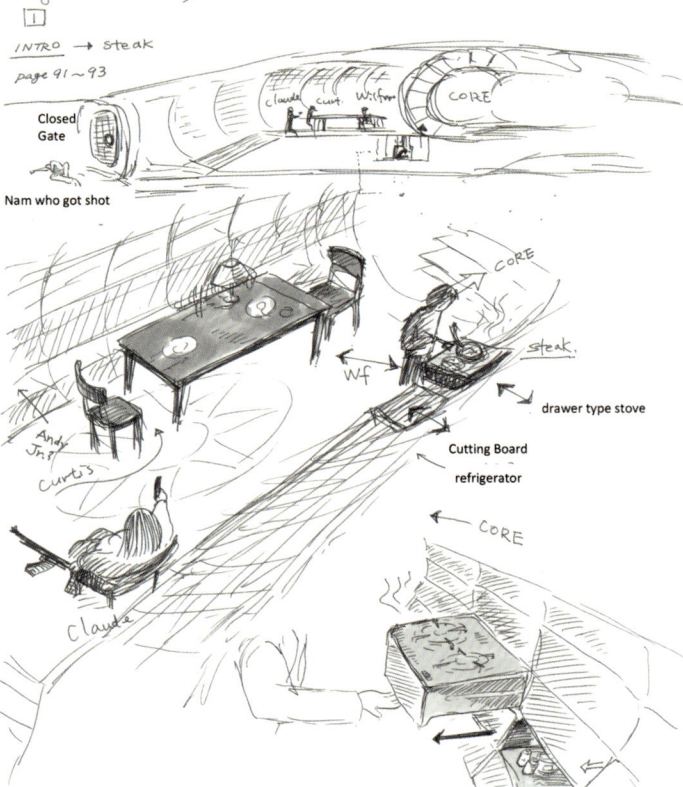

As with every other train car, there has to be a reality to it, some psychological truth. Whether the audience ever know it or not, even the smallest details must hold weight in the *Snowpiercer* universe.

"Wilford lives there," Nekvasil explains. "He can cook there, he can open this drawer and make a bed, he can sit at the table. We didn't show the drawer because we didn't have time to do it, but we drew that he was cooking something and he would open the drawer and there was a hot plate and he'd be cooking something on the hot plate. We thought this whole section would be drawers and he has everything he needs there. That was the basic concept of his space."

These drawers, the utility of the space—a place for everything and everything in its place—all feeds into the psychology of Wilford and everything we have learned about him so far. Everything has its designated space. Who he is—his enforced will—is everywhere. And, just as Curtis discovers, his influence has been present where we the audience might not have even been aware of. Eagle-eyed viewers can go back to the classroom scene and to the documentary shown to the kids to see evidence of it.

"We shot footage for that documentary in Jemniště Chateau near Prague," recalls Nekvasil. "The inlaid wooden floor in that documentary that the boy's sitting on playing with the toy train matches the floor inside the engine room car. That's just a little detail. There's a shared design of the young kid playing with the train and these circles in the parquet floor and the pattern inside his personal space as a grown man. I know it's a little bit cliché, but it's like our *Citizen Kane* [1941]."

ABOVE AND RIGHT Planning every detail from the blocking and the exact placement of the kitchen equipment to the Wilford-branded phone. **BELOW** Director Bong gets hands-on with the set. "The engine itself was pretty much there. There was the rotating part—we did that. We had things moving, so that was CG." —Eric Durst

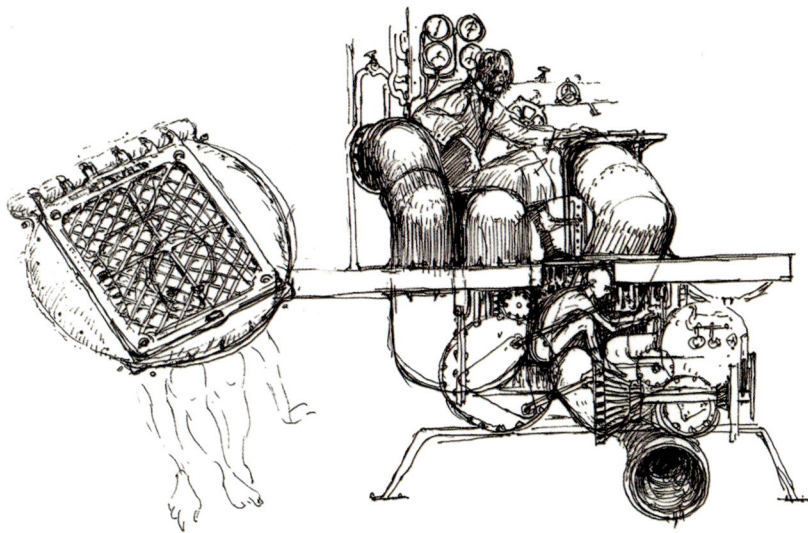

THIS PAGE The discovery of the child slaves, from minutely detailed pencil drawings to finished film stills.

CHAPTER FIVE:

THE SHOOT

Filming commenced at Barrandov Studios on the 16th April 2012 and finished on the 14th July 2012.

But before shooting even began on the soundstages, a key moment that was entirely dependent on the seasonal weather had to be captured. That day was the 20th March 2012 and was the only bit of filming done on location. It so happened that the very first scene shot for *Snowpiercer* was the ending.

In the closing moments of the film, Yona and Timmy emerge from the wreck of the train into a snowy landscape—not a desolate, dead Earth but rather a virgin one. After the darkness, the oppressiveness, and the metallic, industrial nature of the train, the effect of this bright, white, fresh world is visually and emotionally exhilarating. Due to the fortuitous decision to base the production out of Prague, it meant they had an ideal location on the continent. But that still did not mean it would be easy to get to—or to plan for all the variables.

"There was a really big discussion, and it was a crucial moment for production," remembers Ondřej Nekvasil. "This movie is 99% on a soundstage and there's one person in the last scene, which is on location. To be sure we'd have the snow, we'd have to go to Austria and the Hintertux Glacier. We found a good spot, about 2,500 meters above sea level. The producers said, 'Guys, this is so risky. What if you build a big green screen, and the flipped train set on the backlot instead? We'll put fake snow everywhere and use visual effects.' That was a really tricky moment and there was big pressure on Director Bong. He was thinking about that because there was a real sense that we were going just for one shooting day only, and if we go there and the weather is bad, there's no reason to be up there. He really insisted that he would like to shoot outside on the snow and see the snow and see the real nature, even though we had to erase some skiers and some details from the picture. But in general, it was a real space."

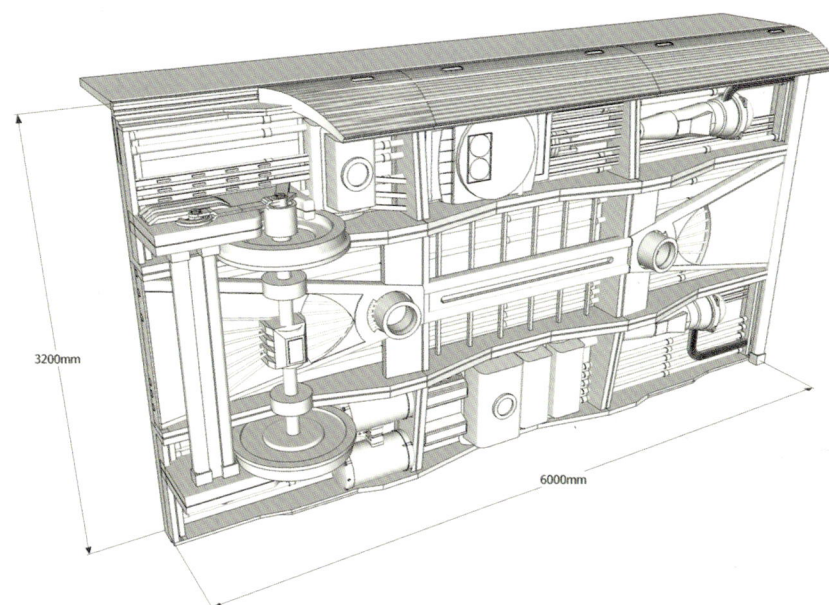

ABOVE AND BOTTOM LEFT A detailed blueprint showing the underside of the crashed train, compared with the finished prop piece transported onto the mountain.
LEFT Concept art showing the Snowpiercer, finally brought to a stop.
BELOW "Director Bong is happy that we finished our first shooting day of *Snowpiercer*!" —Ondřej Nekvasil

① CKD

Slow Track In

Yona picks up a burnt fur coat
(coat from the Opium Den)

② CKD "or"

Location

③ CRRRK!   Yona's feet gently lands on the snow

④ CGI Train   Track Out + Pan Right

Track Out

Train's Bottom CGI

Yona catches Tim crawling down the train   Yona and Tim walks toward the camera

⑤ All White

⑥ Polar Bear?

⑦ Left Tracking + Crane Down

ADULT TIM (V.O.)
I've been cold since the day I was born. Because I was born on the snow.

⑧

⑨ the end.

More to the front than in the drawing

EO.04:0516

EO.04:0516 6560+10

Grand mountain range

Avalanche scene

CGI

CGI Train

Green or Blue Box.
(on location)

① ②

① Background mountain could be composited, however, real image preferable

②

bluescreen on location (?)

CGI railroad.

S# 71
SNOW FIELD

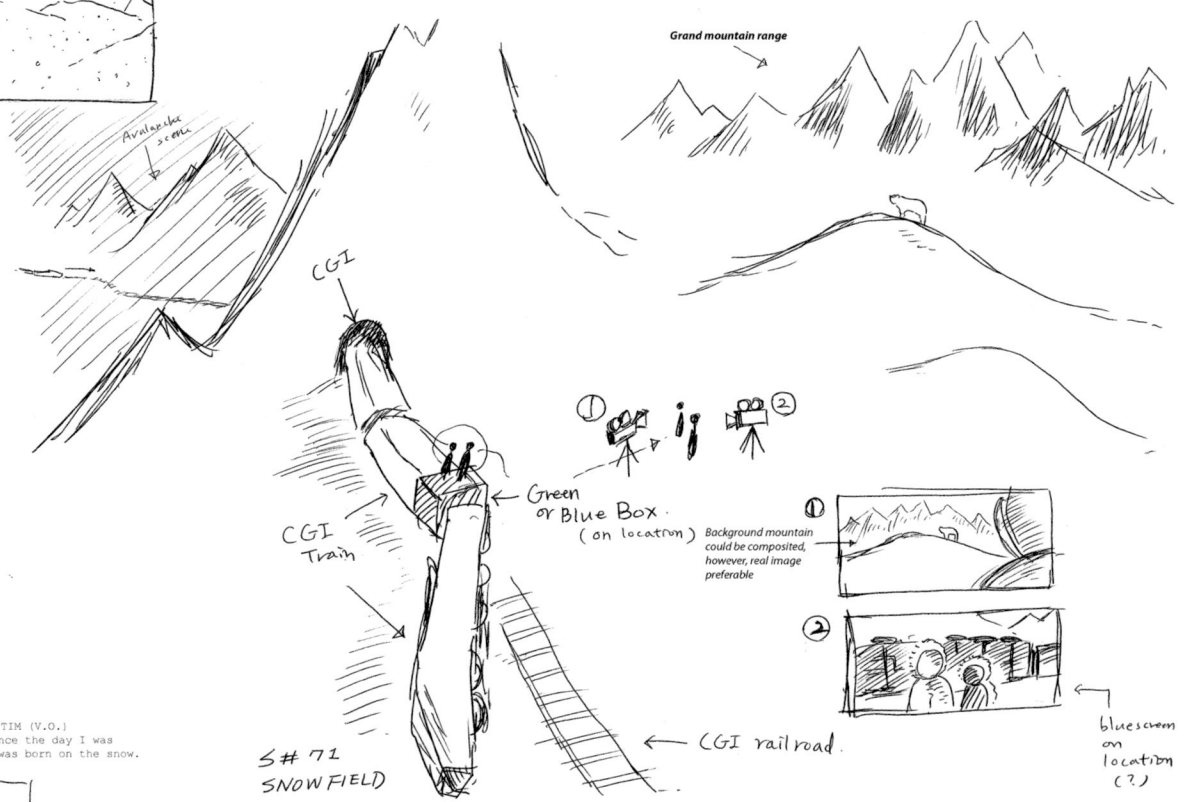

THIS SPREAD "It only comes a few times in life, where you have a director who is prepared, who is ready, who has great ideas, a great script and he's also professional and he's also a wonderful human being. This is the kind of thing that is not often altogether." —Ondřej Nekvasil

EO.04:0516 6601+14

EO.04:0516 6669+05

"EVERYTHING YOU SEE IN THE LAST SCENE OF THE MOVIE WAS THERE. IT WAS REALLY TRICKY FOR DIRECTOR BONG BECAUSE THE PRESSURE ON HIM WAS ENORMOUS. AT THE TIME, IT WAS THE MOST EXPENSIVE MOVIE IN KOREA."

ONDŘEJ NEKVASIL

On the set, everything would be under control, from lighting to exact camera placement. But when shooting on location, there was only so much that Director Bong—who plans every shot in advance—could depend upon. The director of photography on the movie was Hong Kyung Pyo, a regular collaborator of Bong Joon Ho's, having also worked together on *Mother* and *Parasite*. Together they have created unforgettable images, which have an understanding of what they are looking to achieve that goes beyond the minutiae of storyboarding.

When it came to moving the production onto a glacier at high altitude and at the mercy of the elements, Nekvasil spoke to Hong about what the plan was for shooting in potentially difficult conditions. "I remember the director of photography

said, 'Usually, I am lucky for the weather,'" recalls Nekvasil. "I was like, 'Okay! Let's do it!' So we did it. I went there first because we had to move all the set pieces up there to 2,500 meters and build a fragment of the flipped train up there. When I arrived, there was such a dense mist. Nothing was visible. You couldn't see your hand. But we were really lucky because the actual shooting day was excellent. We saw everything, all the mountains. Everything you see in the last scene of the movie was there. It was really tricky for Director Bong because the pressure on him was enormous. At the time, it was the most expensive movie in Korea. He insisted on it and I was really happy that it worked well and that the plan worked. Everything was shot on time and everything was there."

INSIDE THE
SNOWPIERCER

"Anything in the whole wide train?" asks Timmy when Curtis is bribing him for his protein bar. To the people on board, the train is the world. There is nothing else. They might as well be on a rocket hurtling through space.

To capture this feeling of containment, of physical and emotional constriction, the filmmakers decided that as much as possible, filming should take place within each train car set, with the side walls, ceiling, and floor in place. We, the viewer, feel the plight of the tail section survivors and we go on the exact same journey as Curtis through the train.

"What we discussed was how we would shoot there and not expose the fact that we are on a set," explains Nekvasil. "Usually, there's a rule that if the camera is in the space of the set, you are inside the story, but once the camera goes out, you see the whole set and the immediate effect is, 'Okay, now someone else is looking.' You are not there in the

train. But technically, of course, it's always good to have a chance to open the walls and be able to have a camera crew outside. What we did was build the structure of the cars in a way that we could move the walls to the side and open the cars up and be able to lay parallel tracks inside, so we were able to move with the characters from left to right."

The left-to-right movement of the camera and of Curtis is fundamental to *Snowpiercer*. Curtis is determined to get to the front of the train at all costs. Throughout the movie, we see him continually making choices between left and right, with those options symbolizing life or death, humanity or the engine. Without the need to use words, we the viewers understand the moral choice Curtis is facing—as well as underlining the entire propulsion of the story—every time we see the left/right predicament. Giving us both character development and story in a single frame is one thing, but throughout his films,

Bong Joon Ho has created rules, motifs, and patterns that offer visually impactful drama over the course of the entire movie—every single frame.

"I do like to shoot profile shots," says Director Bong, "but with *Mother* and *Snowpiercer*, the context is very different. With *Mother*, you see a lot of profile shots with the son because when you're looking at the right side of a person's face, you're not able to see his left side. It indicates that there is this hidden half of the character. And in *Mother*, you also have this shot where the angle itself is bent forward—the son covers half of his face with his hand and I think that really showed the intention I had with the profile shots in that film.

"With *Snowpiercer*, the energy of the film depended on and was driven by this obsession to move toward the right side of the screen. You only find out later on in the story that there were these characters who are trying to go outside of this train. Until the middle of the film, it's really about this obsession to go to the front, and I think that the energy that comes from that sense of direction really depended on Chris's eyes and face that you see in those profile shots. So I just ended up shooting a bunch of shots of Chris Evans's right cheek. It was really hard to see his left cheek!"

LEFT "In the movie, on the screen, left side is the back of the train, right side is the front, so when Curtis says, 'We're going to the front,' he's going from the left of the screen to the right, and we really tried to maintain that sense of direction and that directionality." —Bong Joon Ho
THIS SPREAD "He has a very specific vision. I've never worked with another director who quite shoots the same way Bong does." —Chris Evans

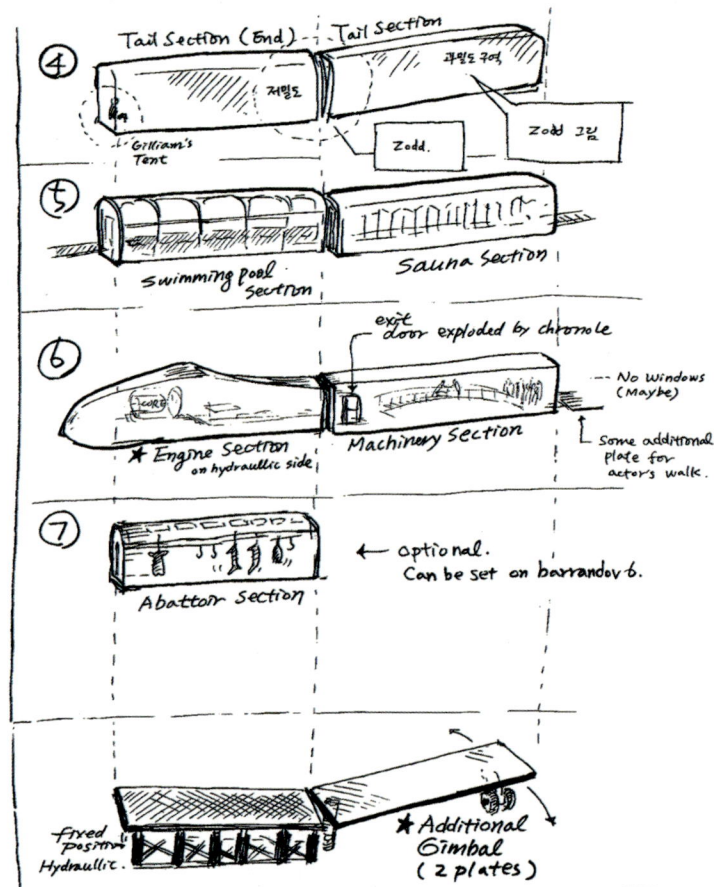

Factory 1
(CKD ?)

④ Tail Section (End) — Tail Section
제밀도
크림도 7열
Gilliam's Tent
Zodd.
Zodd 크림

⑤ Swimming pool Section
Sauna Section

⑥ exit door exploded by chronole
No Windows (Maybe)
★ Engine Section on hydraulic side
Machinery Section
Some additional plate for actor's walk.

⑦ Abattoir Section
← optional. Can be set on barrandov 6.

Fixed position Hydraulic.
★ Additional Gimbal (2 plates)

Factory 2

⑧ GreenHouse Section
Aquarium Section
Sushi Bar

⑨ Guest room Section
Fast movement of camera and characters
Lounge & Beauty salon Section

Fixed 2 sections Without Gimbal

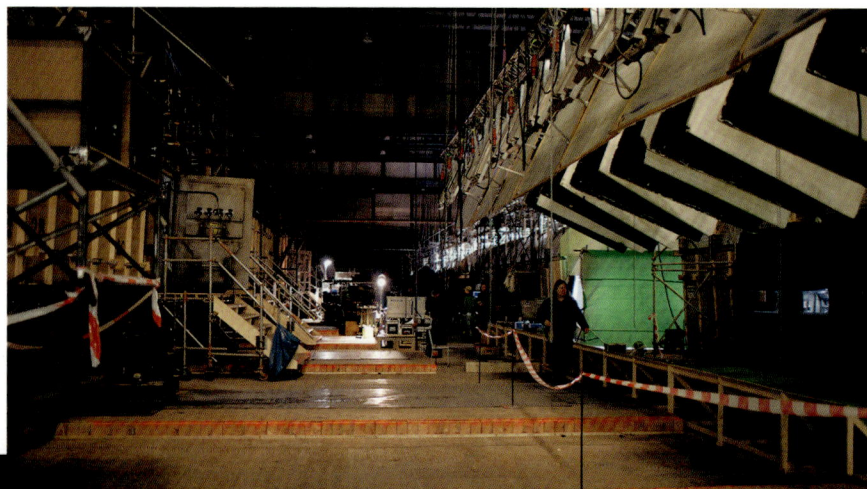

THE SHOOT:
KNOW YOUR PLACE

The film shot mostly in chronological order. The progression of Curtis and his fellow survivors mirrored the progress of the shoot—with the exception being the last scene of the movie. Due to the nature of building all these cars on time and on budget, they had to shoot everything needed in one train car before they moved onto the next. Building the entire train would have been far too expensive and far too big, so the production decided on a schedule: a cycle of building and dressing a set, and while that was being shot on, they would move onto the next one and so on, before returning to the first train car to rework it and start again.

"We built frames, the general structure of the train cars, but only the structure was expensive," confirms Nekvasil. "We were able to reuse it. That was the reason why we were able to go into one stage twice: first it was one type of car, we went to another stage, then another stage, then after four–six weeks, we came back and there was a different car on the same stage. It was very organized. He's [Director Bong] really focused on his work and he spends a lot of time prepping the project. Otherwise, we'd have had to spend much more money building more cars, having more stages, and all of that stuff, which is definitely more expensive for a production and more difficult."

"You had to shoot out one car and then that car was gone and the next car was there," says Eric Durst. "You couldn't go back and catch up because that set was destroyed—revamped into something else."

The production itself was like a train, constantly moving forward, with Director Bong working on the biggest sets for any film he'd made at that point. This massive logistical effort by him and his team was ultimately in service of one thing: the story.

"Early on in the shoot, our shooting schedule was pretty much dominated by the production art department," Bong Joon Ho explains. "They would create a section of the train, and we would shoot all the scenes that take place in that section, and then move on to the set next door, shoot on another train car, and while we were doing that, they would destroy the set we were originally on and then build another set. Physically, it was very difficult coordinating all these different sets, and so our schedule was really dominated by this train set and the art department. At the beginning of the shoot, we shot mainly in the tail section—we weren't even able to see what the cars at the front would look like. Then, while we were shooting in the tail section, we had Tilda appear; this character of Minister Mason, who really represents the whole rich class that resides in that train, in her funky glasses and heavy fur coat. When that character appeared in the tail section, I think it really showed the discrepancy between rich and poor, and how the front cars and the tail cars would clash. I think that's what really excited us, to see that clash, and it meant that we were finally able to witness the tension that this film would contain."

"Ondřej, Dooho, the cinematographer, and I were all quite excited after Tilda's first day when we finally got to see her do the 'Be a Shoe' speech," remembers Bong Joon Ho. "I think that day really defined how this film would feel... She was so fantastic; her performance was amazing. I was so sure that we had created this absolutely unique character that we had never seen before, not in sci-fi films or any films, really, and I felt that so surely on the first day shooting with Tilda. As a film director, there's not much more you can hope for."

Aside from this milestone moment, memories of working with actors on his films come harder to Director Bong. Part of his immense preparation for a film is hiring the right actors and that trust translates into the shoot, where he is able to build the arena for these highly talented performers to work.

"I use very meticulous storyboards and constantly think about the relationship between the camera and actors, the screen ratio and the *mise-en-scène*," he says. "I think those are the basics that you do as a film director, and I have very clear memories about how I came to those decisions, and how I led things on set. But for some strange reason, I don't really remember the sorts of things I discussed with actors and I don't remember what I told them. It just feels that I somehow got through the process and returned to my hotel and have no real specific memories. I just know that I have this very abstract sense of anxiety where I just hope I don't interfere with the actor's process. In Asia, we have the term 'directing acting,' but I think that term in itself is a contradiction."

THIS SPREAD "If you have a line, an exchange with somebody, where the camera happens to be on them and you're off camera, then that line is never going to be on camera, no matter how you perform it... but the inverse is that you also know what part of your performance will be on camera... I've never seen anything else like it and it worked! The proof of whether it did have efficacy or not is the fact that the film is great! So it's a real testament to the conviction and real brilliance of Bong." —Chris Evans

> "THE GOOD THING ABOUT THAT METAL BATTERING-RAM TUBE THING IS IT WAS HEAVY, IT WAS HARD WORK, AND IT WAS DANGEROUS GETTING THROUGH NARROW DOORWAYS. WHAT YOU SEE THEM DOING WAS REAL."

JULIAN SPENCER

One major sequence required of the actors early on is when the tail section inhabitants drive a battering ram through the car and into the next one. With this action, the revolution is finally underway.

This scene features one of the very few moments when the left-to-right directional movement of the film is broken. "Out of the 1200 or so shots in *Snowpiercer*, only three or four had that directionality flipped," Director Bong confirms. "That was because of limitations of space when we were shooting and during the action scenes, but they're very short, so they pass by pretty quickly. Like, for example, you have the tail sectioners attacking the doors with a battering ram, and one of the doors is flipped in that sequence."

The film used a great deal of in-camera effects and strove for reality wherever achievable. Handling the battering ram was no different. "A big challenge on that bloody train was that big battering ram," explains stunt coordinator Julian Spencer. "Somebody beat me to it, because when I got out there, it was being built, and I like to adapt and make it the best you can. I would have asked for a cardboard one but no, they gave us a real metal one, on a train, with men lifting it. I had a lot of injuries with that in rehearsal, picking that thing up and running down with it. We were all glad when those scenes were over as it was all quite hard. Getting Chris jumping up and running down the pipe required lots of little things going on behind the scenes to make it completely safe. A lot of guys wanted to have this piece of rope looped around their wrist, but I'd say no, hands only, because if you go down, you're going to be dragged for six or seven feet before all the men could dig the anchors in and stop it.

"But they didn't have to act. The good thing about that metal battering-ram tube thing is it was heavy, it was hard work, and it was dangerous getting through narrow doorways. What you see them doing was real. The sweat and all the rest of it; the blood and the tears were for real on that because it was a hard thing to do. It was good, though. We got it and it looked incredible. You can see the weight and the heaviness and the awkwardness and the clumsiness of it all. The boys worked hard on that and did very, very well."

Once the characters have broken through, the march—or pilgrimage—to the sacred engine has begun. Handling the battering ram was just the start for both the characters and the actors.

THIS SPREAD Designing, building, and shooting the battering ram. A great deal of work was put into planning and creating this realistic prop. Wherever possible, authenticity and truth were key. "To work with Bong Joon Ho and see what he wanted to portray was just phenomenal. I wish I could work more with him, I really do." —Julian Spencer

THE SHOOT:
BE A SHOE

A masterpiece of staging in a movie filled with motivated camera and character movement, the famous 'shoe speech' scene physically tells us everything the audience needs to know about the plot and the characters, while the dialogue expresses the themes and motivations.

"Passengers, this is not a shoe. This is disorder. This is size ten chaos. This—see this—this is death. In this locomotive we call home, there is one thing that's between our warm hearts and the bitter cold. Clothing? Shields? No! Order! Order is the barrier that holds back the frozen death. We must all of us on this Train of Life remain in our allotted stations. We must each of us occupy our preordained, par-tic-u-lar position. Would you wear a shoe on your head? Of course you wouldn't wear a shoe on your head. A shoe doesn't belong on your head. A shoe belongs on your foot. A hat belongs on your head. I am a hat; you are a shoe. I belong on the head—you belong on the foot. Yes? So it is. In the beginning, order was prescribed by your ticket. First class, economy, and freeloaders like you. Eternal order is prescribed by the *Sacred*

Engine. All things flow from the Sacred Engine. All things in their place, all passengers in their section, all water flowing, all heat rising pays homage to the Sacred Engine... in its own par-ti-cu-lar, preordained position. So it is. Now, as in the beginning, I belong to the front, you belong to the tail. When the FOOT seeks the place of the HEAD, a sacred line is crossed. Know your place! Keep your place! Be a shoe!"

Shoes are made for walking, so despite the fact that Mason explains that they are at the bottom of the pecking order, she is actually unintentionally telling the tail-section passengers to get moving—which they do.

For Ewen Bremner, filming the scene presented its own complications. "It was an operation filming that sequence with the arm going through the hole. I think it was more than a day doing that particular sequence. I have a joint condition that can cause that shoulder to dislocate quite easily, so I told them that if they want to shoot me with that arm through the train at this intended angle, they should really

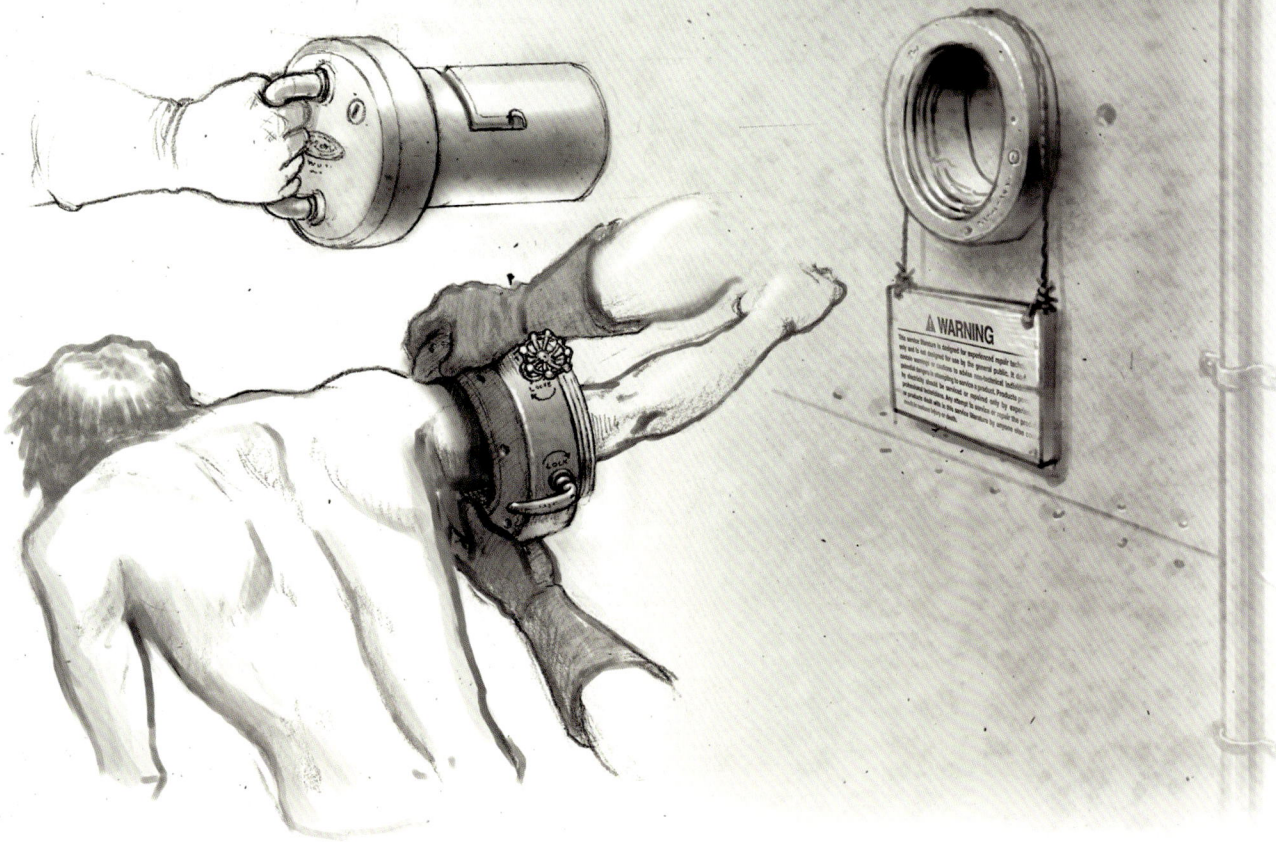

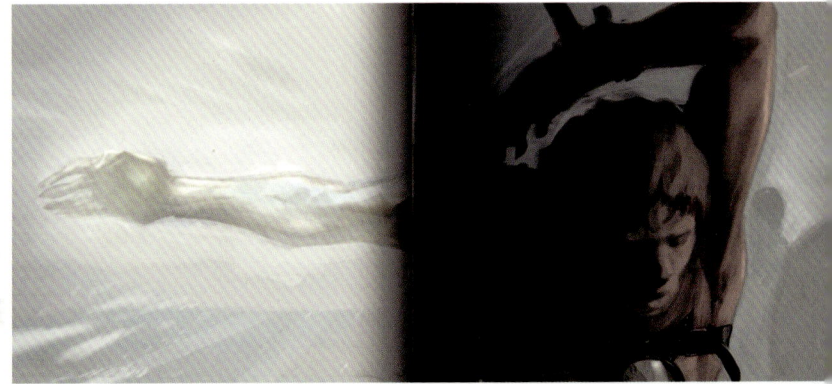

use my left arm, which was totally fine and wouldn't be any problem at all. But my right shoulder is a mess. Because everything is so designed in that film... these carriages had already been conceived, envisioned, and meticulously designed. There's a train full of spectators who are watching this event with Tilda commanding, the shoe on the head, the arm to be removed, stuck out of the train—it had already been conceived and it wasn't possible for them to switch it round so that it would be my left arm that would be removed. That was really challenging, but they were so careful, so respectful, they really looked after me through it to make sure I was safe and that I was not being put in any kind of danger. It was a little bit touch-and-go, but they really bent over backward to make me safe."

ABOVE AND LEFT Plotting and shooting the scene that tells the audience everything we need to know about the situation both inside and outside the train.

THIS SPREAD "In all of his films, [Director Bong]'s seeing how far he can stretch an idea and take it to its conclusion. That takes courage and a strong appetite. And a rigorous intellect to do that, to actually go beyond what is regarded as a safe distance. He'll always go beyond that to see what's on the other side." —Ewen Bremner

THE AXE FIGHT

There is that moment in a hundred yakuza and kung-fu movies when a crowd of henchmen burst into a room and clash with the hero(es) in an orchestrated melee of violence. For *Snowpiercer*'s big fight scene, we have a version of this but played completely differently. It is an action scene but instead of bone-breaking thrills, it is a chilling, brutal, and emotionally charged set piece. Instead of the axe-wielding henchmen exploding into the room in a tidal wave, when our heroes open the door, the masked men are simply stood there, waiting for them.

Hitchcock describes the difference between surprise and suspense and what it does to an audience by giving an example of a bomb we don't know is in the room that suddenly explodes versus a bomb we do know is in the room. "In the first case, we have given the public fifteen seconds of surprise at the moment of the explosion. In the second, we have provided them with fifteen minutes of suspense." (*Hitchcock/*

Truffaut, 1966) Bong Joon Ho presents us and his characters with a train car full of grinning henchmen who are more than ready and willing to take on our rebels, none of whom are trained fighters. Instead of gleefully anticipating the fight, we as the audience are dreading it.

Before the fight commences, we have what is perhaps the most surreal and disturbing image in the film, where the henchmen slit open a fish from fin to mouth and pass it between them, each letting the edge of their blades taste the blood. This moment was famously almost cut by Harvey Weinstein before Director Bong explained that it was a homage to his father—a complete lie. But the scene stayed intact.

When the battle finally begins, it is an unpredictable mass of blood, weapons, and bodies that has more in common with a violent city protest than a blockbuster action scene. This was wholly intentional and to achieve this level of realism, Bong Joon Ho turned to Julian Spencer.

"I did a film many years ago called *Eastern Promises* [2007]," recalls Spencer. "The fight scene that I did for that, Director Bong liked the way it had been put together and the way it was shot. It's what I like to do: more realistic than Hollywood, no fancy frills. It's gruesome, raw, in your face. You can see the passion and the energy going into the punch, rather than ducking and diving and becoming a superman during the fight scene. That never works for me."

Spencer's approach favors natural reactions and improvisation rather than pre-planned stunt work that syncs perfectly with the camera movements.

"My version of putting a fight together is not involving choreography of any kind... If you're stood there for more than two seconds, grab somebody and beat the crap out of them—safely... If the director specifically wants to see, say, a vase being thrown or whatever, I'll say, 'Right, throw the vase, and then in between the vase throwing and shooting something else, just beat the crap out of a person; don't say how, just make it up as you go along.' What I do tend to do a lot of the time is shout at them, shout over the top because there's so much noise in a fight. I'll shout, 'Grab him,' 'Punch him,' 'Kick

him,' 'Throw him,' 'Headbutt,' whatever, make it up as you would do in a real fight. That's what I like to try to get across, so the audience is feeling it with them, rather than seeing a choreographed dance routine which, to me, looks appalling and not believable at all... One of the actors said initially, 'We've got to have choreography,' and I said, 'No, it's not a dance. You are going to get bashed up, bruised, scraped, it's part and parcel. We're going to try our hardest to make sure no one gets hurt. You might get a little bit cut, you've got to be prepared for this to happen, but my guys are there to look after you.'"

Spencer was able to rehearse the axe fight well in advance to find the right look and rhythm but also to ensure everyone felt confident and safe.

"I had six weeks of rehearsals to teach these stunt guys the way I wanted to do it, rather than rehearsing day in day out a specific fight scene. We got the actor in there to teach him how to throw a stage punch, all the stage kicking, punching, falling, where you can make contact with a punch, where you can't, where the danger areas are. Everybody puts that into place, so even the guys who were working close to the camera with the actor, or even the guys who were three or four rows back throwing punches, even then, if you were to focus away from the two in front of the screen and go back to the people at the back, I wanted that to look amazing, too. Generally what happens is they say we'll give you ten stunt men and twenty extras and I say I don't want that because the extras will ruin the filming. All the fighters on that train were stunt men, so I had the same level of aggression and violence working for the people in close to the camera and the people behind them, and the people behind them, and the people behind them, to the back of the train. That way, the levels of aggression were still there, rather than, 'Oh let's just do this and then pick our noses because no one can see us because we're background,' which is what you get with supporting artists sometimes, because they're not fighters, they're not trained."

THIS PAGE "Even his fights are authentic and raw and messy. We're not doing these choreographed fight sequences. It's brawling, so you really just want to let the cameras roll and see what you can come up with." —Chris Evans

OPPOSITE PAGE "I remember Jamie asking me what kind of performance he ought to give and I gave him quite a simple answer, I told him that you are incredibly scared, your face is filled with fear but your body automatically goes forward, whether that is because of fate or instinct or because the character is just following the lead of Curtis, your face is overcome with fear but your body just heads forward toward the soldiers with the axes." —Bong Joon Ho

For some actors this was a different fighting style than they were used to, but it suited the film. Chris Evans, who is the focal point of the fight, threw himself into the rumpus, fighting as Curtis would rather than as Steve Rogers would.

"I had worked with Chris Evans a couple of years before on a film called *Sunshine*," says Spencer, "so I knew he was a very capable man, incredibly fit and healthy. He can just do it: you speak to him once and he's just on his way and doing it... Chris would walk on set, in a good mood, a bad mood or whatever mood, and he'd just switch on and say to me, 'How many?' and I'm giving him about six of my guys. We had about twenty-five to thirty guys in that sequence, and I just said 'Six of the guys are going to get in front of you, just kill them. You can kill them, punch them, throw them, do whatever you like.' He asked which six and I said, 'I don't know.' You get a very raw-looking scene. In a real fight, you haven't got a clue who the next person is or what's going to be thrown at you, and that's what I like to try to portray on film. Chris loved it as much as the stunt boys did. It keeps everyone on their toes. Continuity-wise, it's a pain in the ass because it changes each time, but that's the style of fighting I like to do."

The filming of the fight sequence was a safe space and as with filming any kind of physically intimate scene, trust was paramount. Jamie Bell recalls how that sense of trust channeled through the whole crew, led by Director Bong.

"I can't remember if it was me or one of the other actors who had to do a stunt," says Bell. "Someone had to come up and flip onto their back, and I think there was a little hesitancy about doing it. They said, 'How am I going to do this, how does it work?' I remember there was this back pad and Director Bong just put the back pad under his T-shirt and said, 'You know, something like this,' and he did this incredibly quick, high-off-the-ground, violent slam onto his back, and all of us were like, 'Eeeeeek.' Everyone laughed, and he was laughing, and everyone was amazed that he'd done it. He said, 'Something like that.' His philosophy was if you need to do it, I'll do it."

As much as any other scene in the film, the axe fight tells a story. It is a visceral and thrilling set piece. For Curtis, there is something cathartic in the combat and bloodletting, but he does not let it halt his constant pushing toward the front of the train. Nothing will stop his progress, as we see in the most heart-wrenching moment of the film. Edgar is seized by Franco the Younger, who holds a knife to his throat, and Curtis must choose between his best friend and pursuing Minister Mason.

He chooses Mason.

"I was very honest with Bong," explains Jamie Bell. "Edgar was meant to have his throat slit in a really gruesome, eyeball-bulging kind of way. I said, 'I don't know how to act this. I don't know how to act getting your throat slit.' The other thing I really genuinely felt is that it doesn't feel noble, and I wanted his character to have his nobility, because he was such a freedom fighter, such a revolutionary, I wanted it to feel like he really tried, like he was trying until the very end. There was something that felt so oppressive about this and I didn't want to give that to the oppressors, I wanted him to be fighting to the very last second. Bearing in mind everything about Director Bong's shooting style—very structured, very prepared, everything is on a storyboard, everything is to the minute—I was terrified because I don't know how to alter the machine to get him to do it a different way, if that's even possible.

"I'd worked with Spielberg, I'd worked with Eastwood, but still I didn't feel like I'd found my voice where I could really change a director's opinion about how he's going to approach shooting a movie. I always knew that if you're going to try to change something, you have to offer something up, you have to offer something that's either better or just different. I just came out with this idea that he feels trapped—you have that eyesight connection to Curtis—and that he's trying until the end, he manages to squirrel away and then you're on his face when you know that he feels it's really over. Bong really listened to me, and he took it all on and it's in the movie.

"It clearly resonates with people now because it's true to the character, and there's so much other gruesomeness in the movie. Just the fact that he was so willing to change, willing to listen, made me feel again like an equal, that we're all in it together. It's just one of those extraordinary actor-director relationship moments where you don't forget it, because it's someone who didn't have to say yes. He's the director and if he'd said this is the way, I'd have said, 'It's your vision and I absolutely respect you and trust you,' and I would have done it. I just find it absolutely amazing and I'm still kind of indebted to him... That was the moment where you feel so connected, and so grateful that you're given the space to do what you do. And I think it really works in the film, I really do. It feels like a tragic end to that character and it connects him and Curtis in a way that Curtis is now carrying for the rest of the movie, and that was an important step. All credit to Bong for letting me have that moment."

Julian Spencer agrees, "It was one of the best dying scenes I've ever seen."

"I LIKE TO DO A FIGHT WITH A GOOD STORY TO IT. IT'S GOT TO HAVE A REASON."

JULIAN SPENCER

THE GIMBAL

SNOWPIERCER GIMBAL DESIGN
by director Bong Joon Ho

Note: the illustration has been imagined according to reenact the requisite movement of the train according to the Director without professional knowledge for such equipment.

Barrandov
Max Stage (8, 9, 10)

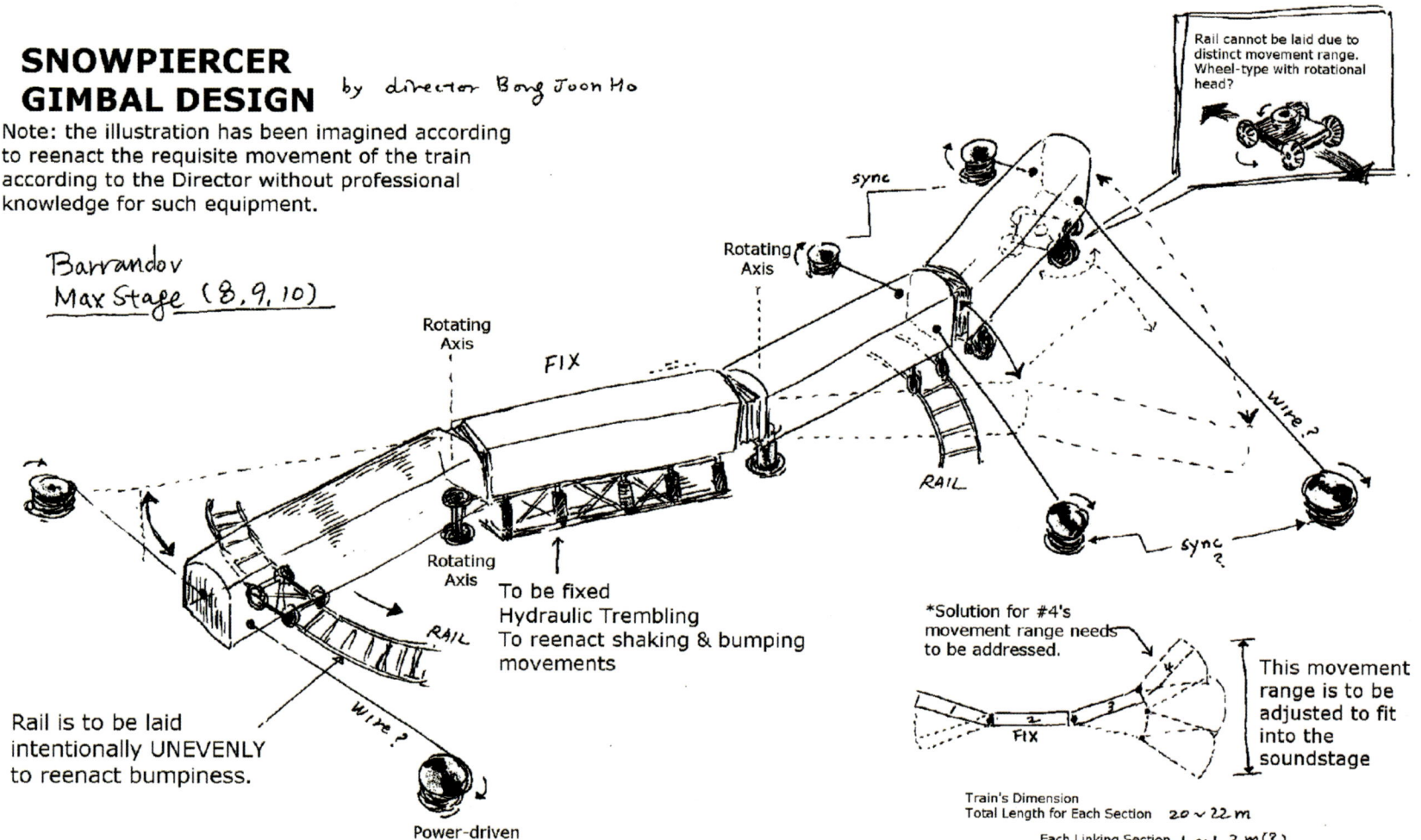

Rail cannot be laid due to distinct movement range. Wheel-type with rotational head?

sync

Rotating Axis

Rotating Axis

FIX

Rotating Axis

RAIL

wire?

To be fixed
Hydraulic Trembling
To reenact shaking & bumping movements

sync?

Rail is to be laid intentionally UNEVENLY to reenact bumpiness.

RAIL

wire?

Power-driven

2011.9.9
From Bong

*Solution for #4's movement range needs to be addressed.

FIX

This movement range is to be adjusted to fit into the soundstage

Train's Dimension
Total Length for Each Section 20 ~ 22 m

Each Linking Section 1 ~ 1.2 m(?)

$$(20 \sim 22) \times 4 + (1 \sim 1.2) \times 3 = \text{Total Length}$$

$$83 \sim 91.6\ m$$

For sets and VFX, the movie was a combination of CG and in-camera practical effects. One of the most significant pieces of technology utilized was the gimbal: an enormous rig for the carriages to sit on, which would recreate the motion of an actual train.

"Director Bong wanted to see the thing move. You needed that extra movement to sell the fact that you were on a train," explains Dooho Choi. "The gimbal was essential. Each train car was twenty-five meters long, and we had four of them built on the gimbal. We'd shoot those sequences and go to another set while we broke down the first four sets and put another four cars on the gimbal. The other cars we shot weren't on the gimbal, so only a certain number of sets actually moved. Gimbals are expensive and often don't work properly, so there were concerns that it would be a big waste of money, but it worked beautifully and we never once had an issue."

It is, of course, not about creating an approximation of movement to occur randomly. Which cars are moving when and in what manner has to be perfectly planned and exactly replicated so that multiple shooting takes match, so the footage cuts together as planned according to the angles and rhythm that Bong Joon Ho had storyboarded.

"We had these four train cars, which were on a gimbal, which was able not only to shake with the cars but also to move the cars into a curve," describes Ondřej Nekvasil. "When you see the car turning to the right or left, we were able to make that effect. There were four cars connected together, able to move like that and also in the same moment to shake. The floor support, the metal structure, all that technical structure and effects—that was really a very complex set. We built the structure and were trying to recycle that set two or three times for the different cars, just to get the movement. Originally, Director Bong was looking forward to having more cars on the gimbal but it was so expensive that we couldn't do it with every car. At one

point, he cut some gimbals because he said there was no need to have gimbals for these certain cars. But we were able to do at least one set of the cars with moveable action and make the feeling of the rumbling train."

This gimbal added a layer of verisimilitude that helped sell the notion of being on a real train to both the actors and, eventually, the audience. But not everyone found this level of authenticity beneficial.

"The worst thing they ever did was putting one of the carriages on a gimbal," says Julian Spencer, who at one point tried to choreograph the axe fight on a gimbal-assisted car. "We had motion sickness, and it would put people off. We just said stop, we can't do that unless we spend another month acclimatizing everybody to motion and then practicing our fight routines. It wasn't going to work because it was incredibly left to right, left to right, bouncing as people overact sometimes walking down the train. People were being sick! There were no windows. It just wasn't very good."

THIS SPREAD "I really wanted a set that would move like a snake, that would have all these joints that twist and turn, and Ondřej had the solution to creating such a moving set." —Bong Joon Ho

Marco Beltrami is an industry veteran, having composed over ninety scores for film and TV, spanning everything from westerns to superhero blockbusters. He has been nominated for Academy Awards® and won an Emmy® for his and Brandon Roberts' work on the documentary *Free Solo* (2018). *Snowpiercer* is the only one of Director Bong's films that is scored by an American composer, so the relationship with Beltrami is unique to that film. But as with everything about the film, the process of creating the score was unconventional.

Often—and especially on big-budget and large-scale movies—a composer is brought on toward the end of the filmmaking process: the movie is all but complete and the music is one of the last elements after every other decision has already been made. However, Beltrami was contacted by Director Bong before a single frame had been shot.

"It was a year before the project started shooting, actually," recalls the composer. "He was doing meetings to set up the movie and we met at the Beverly Hills Hotel, had lunch together, and he had drawings for different scenes and was just talking to me about what the movie was going to be. I was really, really curious. After that, I read the comic and script, and our relationship started by him asking me to send over music

that this [*Snowpiercer*] inspires—previous things I'd done." Samples Beltrami sent included two of his scores for director Alex Proyas: *I, Robot* (2004) and *Knowing* (2009), which provided an entry point for the direction they wanted *Snowpiercer* to head in. Beltrami explains, "There were a couple of propulsive pieces in there that I think he responded to. Music is so abstract and people have a hard time talking about it, so to have a familiarity and to understand what it is that he's responding to early on, I think that was such a great idea because then you're not jumping off cold. You're ready. You have a vocabulary between the two of you."

Fundamental to this vocabulary was establishing the ideas of the score. Every part of a Director Bong film feeds into the central themes and conceits, so the music has to be as philosophically apiece as the cinematography or set design, and is in no way incidental.

"We spoke about the core concepts, musically, and there were basically three: the concept of this perpetual engine, which would also be the energy, the propulsion that would go through the score; there was a thematic idea for the character Yona; and then there was also music for the outside world—the icy outside world. Those were the main thematic things I tried to develop."

The marketing for the movie and a quick, one sentence premise paints *Snowpiercer* very much as a sci-fi film, but just as *Snowpiercer* does not feel 'futuristic' in its style or design, neither does its music.

"I never really conceived of it as being sci-fi," says Beltrami. "The movie to me never seemed that sci-fi. And the movie is always the driving force as to what the score is going to be. I was just trying to be in concert with the film."

He goes on to list what was used on the soundtrack, "I had thirty strings, a harp, and a piano, two flutes, two clarinets, four horns, three trombones, a tuba, a timpani, and three percussionists. It was a pretty decent-sized group... It was a very orchestral score. There were some acoustical sounds that we manipulated to become timbres that were unique. Metallic sounds were used in the axe fight but, for the most part, it was more orchestral."

THIS SPREAD "It was a very collaborative relationship, which is very rare for most movies I do. Usually, I get hired when the movie is complete, given two or three months, but this was really great because you could really explore stuff. I already had an idea of what was in his ear in terms of things you're aspiring to musically: cambers, sounds, harmonies, rhythmical things. It gave me a jumping-off point." —Marco Beltrami
OPPOSITE RIGHT Sheet music for 'This is the Beginning' by Marco Beltrami.

> ## "I REMEMBER THE FIRST SCENE HE SENT ME WAS THE BEGINNING OF THE AXE FIGHT WHEN THEY GO TO OPEN THE DOORS AND THERE'S ALL THOSE GUYS STANDING THERE. THAT WAS THE FIRST PIECE I WORKED ON."
>
> MARCO BELTRAMI

The axe fight is a moment of collision on this journey. It is when so much crashes together: oppression and revolution, anger and sadness, civilization and brutality. And the music and sound design are blurred in this sequence, bleeding into one another and creating a weight of emotion and drama that unnerves as much as the sight of the grinning masked men.

"I remember the first scene he sent me was the beginning of the axe fight when they go to open the doors and there's all those guys standing there," recalls Beltrami. "That was the first piece I worked on. We sampled all these metallic percussive sounds and combined that with some orchestral stuff. There was a pump organ

I used because the bellows have such a noisy sound, like breathing. Director Bong really liked it. He said it reminded him of a rock band. John Bonham, I think. He meant that it has so much energy to it, so that was really inspiring... We used the score for those moments when the scene opens up, then when the axe fight continues later on into this slow motion, over-the-top, bloody thing, I remember the sound effects being very stylized as well. It wasn't supposed to be a realistic type of thing but more hyper stylized. The music at that point becomes very subdued—it's just like a piano. I think I just used a couple of instruments. That's actually probably one of my favorite sequences in the movie."

WHAT HAPPENS IF THE ENGINE STOPS?
WE ALL FREEZE AND DIE.
BUT WILL IT STOP, OH WILL IT STOP?
NO, NO!
CAN YOU TELL US WHY?
THE ENGINE IS ETERNAL,
YES!
THE ENGINE IS FOREVER,
YES!
RUMBLE, RUMBLE,
RATTLE, RATTLE.
WHO IS THE REASON WHY?
WILFORD!
WILFORD, WILFORD, HIP HOORAY!

THIS SPREAD "Bong wrote the lyrics, so I took that and basically wrote the little hymn and had the kids sing. I sent that to him and then he played that on the set and the woman that played the schoolteacher [Alison Pill], she did a great job of playing it on the set. I think they had a bunch of kids sing it. It was really fun. That was before they started shooting." —Marco Beltrami

The big action sequence in the film may have been the first footage from the movie that Beltrami scored, but it was not the first scene he had worked on. "When he was about to start shooting, [Director Bong] mentioned that the first thing they needed, because it was on-screen, was the kids singing in the school car. I said, 'Okay, but where am I going to get these school kids?' So I recruited my whole family to come in and sing: I had little kids at the time. They sang on it and we produced it, I played it on the piano, and I sent it to him. I think they ended up replacing it, but I put a little bit on the soundtrack. That was fun."

The score, like the movie itself, is filled with a diverse combination of elements, ideas, and inspirations. As the cast, the design, and the tone is varied, so is the music. It takes the audience on an aural journey via orchestral pieces, nursery rhymes, and almost heavy-metal sounds, leading eventually to one of the emotional peaks in the film. When Curtis reaches the end of his journey, he is asked by Wilford how long it's been since he was by himself. Wilford leaves him and Curtis has a few moments of solitude with the sacred engine—the place becoming almost a private chapel. The music helps to communicate the feeling of quietness, calm, and personal spirituality.

The track is called 'Take My Place' and Beltrami explains its conception and execution, "It's definitely very emotional. For that scene at the end, I had an organ sound, which I thought was an interesting texture to use with the strings. Maybe it was almost like the engine was a church—the holy space of the train. I had a lot of fun crafting that whole ending part of the movie. It's very symbolic. That's one of the great things about it. Also, it was fun to contrast that with the stuff that's going on right outside the engine car."

The route the train is on is circular, the phases of civilization are circular, and, similarly, the score is circular. The end song, 'This is the Beginning,' could easily be mistaken for an opening credits track; it has perhaps the most drive and propulsion of any piece on the score and, ironically, it's playing now that the train has come to a stop.

"Director Bong had a great concept that the music at the beginning of the movie should be the music of the end, and that the music at the end of the movie should be like the music of the beginning. Meaning that this is sort of like the end of civilization at the beginning of the movie, and then the hope of a new beginning at the end of the movie. I think that was a great concept."

Fittingly, Beltrami's final task on the movie concerned the opening track, 'This is the End,' closing the loop on what had been a two-year process. "One of the early things that I came up with was actually the music for the very beginning when they're talking about the end of civilization and all of that. I took that idea and developed it and built it into a concert piece, so when the movie premiered in Los Angeles—I think it was by the Dolby Theater downtown—before the movie started, we had a live performance of it. I turned that piece into a five-minute little concert suite. I think you can still find it online somewhere. To me, that part was really inspiring and I had a lot of fun."

THE SHOOT:
BONG JOON HO'S SHOOTING STYLE

"Bong is a very interesting and a very unique director. He is just so clear about what he's thought through. He's done his homework ten times over and it's just such a privilege to work with someone like that," Eric Durst says.

On *Okja*, Director Bong stated that, "The way it was written, the way it was storyboarded, and the way it was planned, that was pretty much how I executed the film... I said I needed about 300 *Okja* shots and the final shot count is 295." On *Parasite*, he blocked out character positions and the design of the Park family home during the scripting process. His specificity is one of the many factors that define a film such as *Snowpiercer* as authored unquestionably by Bong Joon Ho. The attention to detail encompasses the smallest actions or the largest ideas—sometimes linking both.

> ## "I LIKE TO TAKE PHOTOGRAPHS OF PEOPLE'S HANDS. TILDA'S HANDS, FOR SOME REASON, WERE VERY MEMORABLE."
>
> BONG JOON HO

"I'm always fascinated by actors' hands," explains Director Bong. "I like to take photographs of people's hands. Tilda's hands, for some reason, were very memorable. She has these long fingers. You can see these hand scenes in *Mother* and *Memories of Murder*, but I paid careful attention to Tilda's hands and tried to think what I could have her do while giving the 'Be a Shoe' speech. Even while writing the script, I kept thinking about where that movement comes from, where I came up with the idea."

Here, he is discussing the mechanical-style movement Mason makes with her hand as she recites the words "particular, preordained position." It is deliberate, significant, and vaguely threatening.

"This part passes really quickly, so it may be difficult for audiences to catch," Director Bong continues, "but that hand movement is repeated by Ed Harris at the end. He crouches down and does that hand movement and he's actually imitating the movement that Timmy is doing inside the engine. Timmy continually repeats the movement in the engine to remove the by-products with his own hand. There was a train malfunction, and the train was unable to supply the new part, so they decided to put in children to continuously remove the by-products with their own hands. Ed Harris is imitating that movement and Tilda, who has met the character Wilford, is repeating the same movement, as if it were a sort of ritual."

Timmy is removing by-products with his hand via the movement. It serves a simple and necessary purpose. By imitating this exact action when disciplining the tail section, Mason is by extension identifying them as the by-product, the waste, that has to be managed in order to keep the train running smoothly.

"HIS PROTOCOL IS UNIQUE AND DID, IN THE BEGINNING, STRIKE US ALL AS A BIT OF A CHALLENGE, BUT IT WAS REALLY REFRESHING ULTIMATELY."

EWEN BREMNER

PREVIOUS PAGE Minister Mason performing the signature hand gesture.
THIS SPREAD "He's a team player, he's one of us, he's getting his hands dirty with you. From an acting standpoint, and probably from a crew's standpoint, it endears you to that person so much because he's in the trenches there fighting with you, he's not behind a monitor, he's not screaming at you through a loud-speaker." —Jamie Bell
OPPOSITE TOP LEFT Director Bong and production designer Ondřej Nekvasil checking the sample of the engine set.
OPPOSITE BOTTOM When Bong Joon Ho first met Tilda Swinton at the Cannes Film Festival in 2011. Photo taken by Sandro Kopp.

With the exception of Song Kang Ho and Ko Asung, the principal actors had not worked with Bong Joon Ho before and found the process unlike any other shooting experience they'd previously had. Ewen Bremner explains, "Normally when you shoot a film, a conventional scene will be broken down into a master shot, a live shot, maybe a profile shot, maybe some cutaways, maybe some close-ups—maybe a dozen shots that the scene will be broken down into. Most of these will be shot from the beginning to the end of the scene, and then an editor gets all of that material and then makes a patchwork from all these different shots to kind of build the scene from those building blocks. Each of those shots will generally run for the length of the scene. But the way Director Bong works, he storyboarded each scene very specifically with a different image for each sentence almost, so each sentence that somebody was speaking was composed of a completely different shot, and he would only shoot that sentence, or couple of sentences, and break everything down and move onto the next image. It might be a long shot, it might be a close-up, it might be a surreal cutaway to somebody's fingertip—it could be anything. Each of the shots were preconceived and will then be executed by him and his cinematographer.

"The actors were quite disorientated at first because we're not used to working in that way, we're used to having a run at the scene from beginning to end, getting that energy flow. But most of the time, we'd be working in the middle of the scene, then he'd rewind to the beginning of the scene and we'd shoot that sentence, then we'd jump forward to the end of the scene, then we'd fill in all the cracks with these different shots and different sections of the scene. It was really revolutionary for all of us, I think. We'd never worked in that way. It was a complete surprise and it did take some getting used to. But there was also a lot about his filmmaking that we had not witnessed before. His protocol is unique and did, in the beginning, strike us all as a bit of a challenge, but it was really refreshing ultimately. I think that if it was a colder director, some of the actors might have got into a bit of a huff about it, but the goodwill that he engenders is so huge."

It is all part of his preparation. Understanding precisely what needs to be done inspires not only confidence in his cast and crew but makes the whole production more efficient.

"It's about economy," says Jamie Bell. "He knows *This is what I need, and I understand how this is going to fit into everything else that I have.* If it's just a tight on me, we don't run the entire scene tight on me, he just explains that for this particular moment, I have to hold out my hand and say this line. I'm sure, by the way, that if you did say, 'I need to do the entire scene to feel that moment,' then he would give it to you. He's not a tyrant, it's not a dictatorship. He loves his actors. He and Tilda had an incredible, special relationship—a loving, trusting, nurturing relationship—and that was just something to behold."

Bong Joon Ho has developed an almost preternatural understanding of behavior and how to communicate it on film—and how to find actors who can also express this. It's why his films are celebrated for being able to navigate changes in tone and even genre from scene to scene and also why *Parasite* won the 2020 Screen Actors Guild Award® for Best Cast—a first for a foreign-language film.

As with all things on a production, Director Bong uses a thoughtful and considered approach to working with actors. Hitchcock may have once said (in his 1965 acceptance speech for his Screen Producers Guild Milestone Award), "Actors should be treated like cattle," but Director Bong does not see them as pieces in the machinery of his movie, like how Wilford would. They are people and it is their story we are watching. Just as the lighting technician or costume designer knows their job, so too does the actor.

"As a director, I think my role is just carefully reviewing the performances that these actors give. Unless you're like Clint Eastwood, who is a director with a ton of acting experience, he might be able to demonstrate himself as a guide. But if that's not the case, I think the best thing a director can do is provide these careful reviews for the actors or perhaps throw in some ideas that they had not thought about themselves. Thankfully, I've always worked with actors whose sense of direction and interpretation for the characters and performances really coincided with my own. I've never had major conflicts with actors and I think part of that is maybe because I cast actors that I know share the same sensibility and can work with me as a great partner. So my experiences with actors have all been quite smooth. I've never got to the point of Herzog and Klaus Kinski...

"I remember this moment at the end of the torch-fight sequence. You have Curtis give up on Jamie Bell's character, Edgar dies, and Curtis runs forward holding this axe to catch Minister Mason, to catch her alive. When we were shooting that scene, Tilda asked me what her character should be doing when Curtis is running toward her. Instinctively, I just told her and started demonstrating that Minister Mason should just point toward him, screaming and cursing, and she really thought this idea was funny. She actually did that and we ended up using it. Thankfully, it suited Minister Mason's character: you have this leader of the revolution running toward you and she's just cussing and screaming. I think what I did was sort of fill in the gaps for an actor; to produce strange ideas that help them fill in the gaps, and as a director, nothing pleases me more than to provide that kind of help."

THIS SPREAD "It was like a magical few months for everyone involved. Everyone has fond memories of that shoot. I'm sure people you're speaking to still get a bit giddy when they think about it all."—Ewen Bremner

The general feeling on set was one of generosity and kinship. Working on a big movie, away from home for weeks or even months, and creating something that had every indication of being quite special, unified the group. So this film about injustice, unfairness, and violent upheaval was borne out of the very opposites.

"It was full of laughs," remembers Ewen Bremner. "I would say the company really socialized a lot more than on any film I've been on. We were always going out for dinner together, or for a late-night drink, or just a walk round town to explore the city, or a yoga class. We were all spending real quality time together.

"Because everyone was out of their element—it was an 'away game' for everybody—there was a sense of camaraderie you don't normally get when people are shooting in LA or London, where everyone goes their separate ways after work. There was a lot of socializing in restaurants and things like that, so we all got to know each other off the clock, which was interesting. John Hurt would write and read his poetry. One night, we were at this restaurant, and John came in and read this poetry that he had written. It was phenomenal."

"We're all the same human beings on a film set," echoes Julian Spencer. "I love being on set. I love being in there and getting hot and sweaty with the fights. I'd shout 'Cut,' and look at Bong and he'd give me that little grin... He gave me a free reign because he obviously appreciated what I love. And yet to stand back and watch him do his stuff as well—to work with someone as fabulous as that—was an absolute pleasure. Not many of them around."

CHAPTER SIX

POSTPRODUCTION

In part due to the proliferation of CGI-fueled blockbusters, there is a misconception that the VFX department only join a project toward the end of the filmmaking process. This is not the case, and certainly not with *Snowpiercer*.

"The VFX is really soup to nuts," explains Eric Durst. "One of the great things about being a VFX supervisor is you get to work with a lot of directors and you are one of the only people who get to work from the first day to the last day. You get to see the whole process of it. Usually the producer is not on, but in this case he was—Dooho was there throughout. It's a rare thing to have people on it from beginning to the end. That's important because there are so many decisions that are made. At the beginning, you can lay it out, but... working with the production designer on what you build and what you don't build—that's a big part of what your preproduction process is. Finding what you need and what you don't need. There are ramifications."

Eric Durst, as VFX designer and VFX producer, had been involved throughout preproduction and shooting, which meant he had been a part of conversations and the thought process. There was an understanding of what they were all striving for and the months of getting used to working together was essential. Durst was responsible for hiring visual effects houses to work on *Snowpiercer* and he knew not only what they had in terms of resource and budget but also the grander creative vision Director Bong was aiming for.

"We had Scanline in Munich," lists Durst. "We had Method in Vancouver, also Method in London. We had UPP in Prague and 4th Creative Party in Seoul. Five houses. We knew [what VFX work was needed in advance]. There are storyboards I have that list the number of VFX shots... We ended up with exactly 1005. There were variations. Sometimes you go to the set and things are a little different than what you planned, and Director Bong is able to think on his feet very quickly, so he alters things if necessary. There were a few things that would happen that were maybe different on the day, then he would change direction a bit. But it wasn't like he came and had a different vision that day and rethought the sequence. It was pretty much working with what reality gives you and altering it but still with the fabric of what he was initially thinking."

Each VFX house was responsible for different elements, with Durst overseeing and distributing the various tasks.

THIS SPREAD The process of bringing the aquarium to life from the green-screen-assisted set to final film still via digital effects.

> "THERE WAS THIS MOMENT WHERE I THOUGHT, *WE'RE NOT SEEING ANY GREEN SCREENS ANYMORE, IT'S ALL THERE, WE'RE ALMOST AT THE END.*"
>
> DOOHO CHOI

"Scanline did all the outside stuff. In broad strokes, Scanline did the avalanche, the train exterior, and a lot of the CG environments. Method in Vancouver did the aquarium and did a lot of similar work for the blue screens outside as well and matched some of the stuff that Scanline had set up for the exteriors. UPP did a lot of various other things. They pre-visualized the train sequence itself and they did a lot of the engine inside—the gears that were moving around and the guy that fell over and got crunched. They did a lot of that. 4th Creative did an enormous amount of work. There was a lot of clean-up stuff that they had to do. A lot of more 'basic' work, but they had a really good eye and some of the stuff was quite difficult... They did very meticulous work and I know people were working around the clock over there."

As with the camera movements throughout the shoot, as with the costumes and the dirt under the nails of the actors, so it goes that there was some fine detail that the VFX teams had to focus on to ensure that the world created on-screen—and the rules within it—held up to scrutiny.

"There were all the environments we see outside the train, of course," says Dooho Choi, "but a lot of the work was just to make things look invisible—wire removals and

set extensions, etc. There were expensive shots and cheap shots; we made a list of the expensive shots and which were really necessary. I remember Director Bong was obsessing over one actor who wore contact lenses, and in a close-up, you could see the outline of the lenses. You wouldn't have contact lenses on that train, there's just no way, so that's the level of detail we were going into."

One of the more VFX-heavy elements of the production was the whole outside world: the frozen Earth that the train endlessly circumnavigates. Except for the end scene, no location shooting was done to conjure the snowy desolation of the dead world. From the ruined cityscapes to the 'Frozen Seven,' everything outside of the train was created through visual effects and much of what is seen outside is, quite simply, snow, and the VFX house was challenged with creating the snow in a realistic and cinematic way.

"Snow is very hard to do because it's white on white on white on white," says Durst. "The color palette is very limited and it's not even black and white, it's just white on white. Shades of white. White can

clip out very easily; if you get a little bit of a line, everything clips out. We were always trying to manage getting enough detail in it. If you look at the film, you can't really understand the level of detail. When you really get in and see how much complexity there was built into the snow and all the different pieces, then you sort of understand how much detail you have to put in to make it look plausible. That was a real challenge.

"Scanline started as the first company who really did water well and that was their ticket to fame. At that stage, maybe fifteen/twenty years ago, you really couldn't do water and they were able to do it very effectively and very well, so that started them on their ride. The same technique for working with fluid dynamics and things like that with water we also used for snow and avalanches, things like that… We were able to have the right people and the right software to work quickly. When you do simulations like this, especially avalanches, often times if you don't have the right software it can take days or weeks to see a version of something. Because Scanline had some very efficient software, which a lot of people have now but they were the only ones in town at that point, they were able to show us iterations pretty quickly, like every day or so. That really enabled us to work in a speedy fashion."

The entire postproduction process was about nine months, from the end of shooting in July 2012 to March 2013. This is fairly typical for a movie of such scale and size.

OPPOSITE PAGE Comparing a pre-CG shot with a finished still shows not only the importance of digital effects but also color grading and how much it alters the mood of a shot.
THIS PAGE "We had, at the end of photography, pretty much the movie. We knew what it looked like. We went back to Seoul to edit and that was, in a way, not really traditional editing. It wasn't like 'I've never seen this before,' it was more refinements and timing and things like that. It was a very different process than you normally would have in editorial."
—Eric Durst

> # "BONG IS SO SPECIFIC ABOUT THINGS. I HAVE A GREAT PICTURE CALLED *LOVE/HATE* AND IT'S BASICALLY A PICTURE OF A SHOT WHERE BONG HAS CIRCLED AND PUT LOVE AND HEARTS ON IT AND WRITTEN HATE ON ANOTHER PART. HE'S VERY DIRECT ABOUT WHAT HE LIKES AND DOESN'T LIKE."
>
> ERIC DURST

After nine months in Prague, it was time for everyone involved to go their separate ways—and yet continue to work together. The crew may have scattered across the world but they found ways to synchronize and liaise to ensure that the same level of care and attention was given as if they were all working from neighboring offices.

"One interesting thing that was different than any other movie I've ever worked on was the editorial process and being able to work remotely," recalls Durst. "It was early days working with Skype and I'd never really worked that way. The fact that we were going to be in L.A. and Bong was going to be in Seoul was a bit of a question mark... The VFX editor, Jinmo Yang, was working with Bong in his apartment. The remote process worked really well. It's commonplace now but at that point it was more rare, especially when the director is overseas and we're here. We would have conversations ranging anywhere from an hour, two hours, to sometimes three hours with Bong in Korea looking at shots, talking about things. We would do that maybe three times a week, then eventually daily. That was the first time I'd—certainly most successfully—experienced working in a remote way that brought this together. I was disappointed because I really wanted to go to Seoul! I've never seen South Korea. But the whole process kept flowing."

One of the reasons it was able to flow so successfully was, again, due to Director Bong's preparation. The editing process went so smoothly, in part, because Bong had been editing for months already—before the shoot had even finished.

THIS PAGE As much preparation as Director Bong does in advance of a shoot, just as much effort is also put into the backend, poring over every single detail, ensuring every frame is part of a unified vision.

"It helped me enormously," confirms Durst. "We had forty-three million dollars but the average Korean movie is maybe two or three million. So this was like a billion dollars for us. It helped me because I could go to the various VFX houses and say, 'I know you put in padding, which you have to because there are going to be changes, things that are going to shift, so you need that buffer just to cover yourself. But in this case, this is very unique—you can trust Bong entirely about what he says he is going to do. He's thought about it. He's already made those variations that usually people make in postproduction after you deliver the shot that you thought was final but now sparks a new idea in somebody. That's usually how it works. This is different. Director Bong has already thought it through and made those considerations. There will be some variations but not much.' We were able to go into this with a very lean budget and hopefully everyone did okay on it— I think they did. It was a straight shot from point A to B, rather than a circuitous route to get there."

The amount of material Bong Joon Ho had been shooting daily in Prague was between 2,500 and 5,000 feet of film. In traditional terms this is, as Durst puts it, "barely anything." He knows exactly what he needs to shoot. The movie he finishes with on celluloid is the movie he started with as storyboards on paper.

This would be crucial when it came to the release.

"You'd do this scene in the morning, come back from lunch and he'd say 'Do you want to see it?'" explains Jamie Bell. "We'd be like, 'What are you talking about?' and he'd say, 'I've cut it already.' I'm someone who hates watching my stuff: I hate watching takes, or scenes, or finished movies, it doesn't help me creatively at all, it stifles me creatively, but I was so curious. Bong clearly knows—he knows how this must work and he's dreamed it, or he's seen it, and sure enough, he's put it together and we watched it. All of it worked! All of it told the story; it was the storyboards in moving images! After that, we just had this infinite trust, this understanding that we are in good hands, safe hands—of someone who knew way more than we did."

What they left Prague with was already an assembled, cut movie. With Jinmo Yang present all through the shoot and with Director Bong sharing the edited footage as it progressed, the postproduction team knew what they were getting when it came time to refine the movie. The months of storyboarding, of planning and executing camera moves, of shooting actors specifically for the compositions he needs all paid off. It was a level of efficiency and economy that served both his vision and the budget.

CHAPTER SEVEN:

THE RELEASE

SNOWPIERCER

FIGHT YOUR WAY TO THE FRONT

The movie had been funded by CJ ENM and when it came time to find US distribution, a deal was made with The Weinstein Company. The Weinstein Company had become a home for filmmakers such as Quentin Tarantino and Anthony Minghella, as well as distributing art-house movies such as Wong Kar Wai's *My Blueberry Nights* (2008) or Derek Cianfrance's *Blue Valentine* (2010), and high-concept filmmaker-led vehicles including *A Single Man* (2009), *The Mist* (2007), and *The Road* (2009). Some films were productions they bankrolled and produced themselves, but others were only distribution deals for certain territories, as was the case with *Snowpiercer*.

Bong Joon Ho likes to have the final cut on all his movies and this proved a problem for Harvey Weinstein, the co-founder of The Weinstein Company, who had his own ideas about what version of the movie should be released to theaters. However, thanks to the fact that Director Bong only shoots what he needs to, there was really only one version of the movie in existence.

"Because Weinstein had money in the game, he wanted to have his own shot at re-cutting it," explains Eric Durst. "But this fits into Bong not shooting any extra footage—it was a puzzle with no extra pieces. If you have a puzzle without any extra pieces, you can only put it together one way. Bong just played it out. At one point, Weinstein wanted it to be twenty minutes shorter and they did the trick of taking three frames off of every shot, that kind of approach. They did all these different versions. In the end, Bong won and got his film the way it should be."

ABOVE What would become the key image in many territories, including the home video release.
RIGHT The French poster. France was one of the first territories outside of Korea to screen the completed movie, with critics from the UK traveling across the Channel to watch it there.

CHRIS EVAN · SONG KANG-HO · TILDA SWINTON · JAMIE BELL · OCTAVIA SPENCER · EWEN BREMNER · ALISON PILL · KO ASUNG · AVEC JOHN HURT · ET ED HARRIS

UN FILM DE BONG JOON HO

SNOWPIERCER
LE TRANSPERCENEIGE

2031. NOUVELLE ÈRE GLACIAIRE.
LE DERNIER REFUGE DE L'HUMANITÉ
EST UN TRAIN.

CJ ENTERTAINMENT PRÉSENTE EN ASSOCIATION AVEC UNION INVESTMENT PARTNERS
UNE PRODUCTION MOHO FILM / OPUS PICTURES UN FILM DE BONG JOON HO "SNOWPIERCER"
CHRIS EVANS SONG KANGHO TILDA SWINTON JAMIE BELL OCTAVIA SPENCER
EWEN BREMNER KO ASUNG AVEC JOHN HURT ET ED HARRIS
CASTING JOHANNA RAY CSA ET ELLEN JEFFRIES CATHERINE GEORGE
MONTAGE SON TAE YOUNG CHOI DIRECTEUR CHANGJU KIM ET STEVEN CHOI
EFFETS SPÉCIAUX ERIC DURST MUSIQUE MARCO BELTRAMI DÉCORS ONDREJ NEKVASIL
DIRECTEUR DE LA PHOTOGRAPHIE HONG KYUNG PYO PRODUCTEURS EXÉCUTIFS PARK DOOHO CHOI BAEK
JISON ADBERT BERNACCHI PRODUCTEURS ÉRIC MIKY LEE
PRODUCTEURS TAE SUNG JEONG STEVEN NAM PRODUIT PAR PARK CHAN-WOOK LEE TAE HUN
D'APRÈS "LE TRANSPERCENEIGE" DE JACQUES LOB BENJAMIN LEGRAND ET JEAN-MARC ROCHETTE
PUBLIÉ PAR CASTERMAN ADAPTÉ POUR L'ÉCRAN PAR BONG JOON HO
SCÉNARIO DE BONG JOON HO ET KELLY MASTERSON RÉALISÉ PAR BONG JOON HO

Le Pacte   CJ ENTERTAINMENT   OPUS pictures

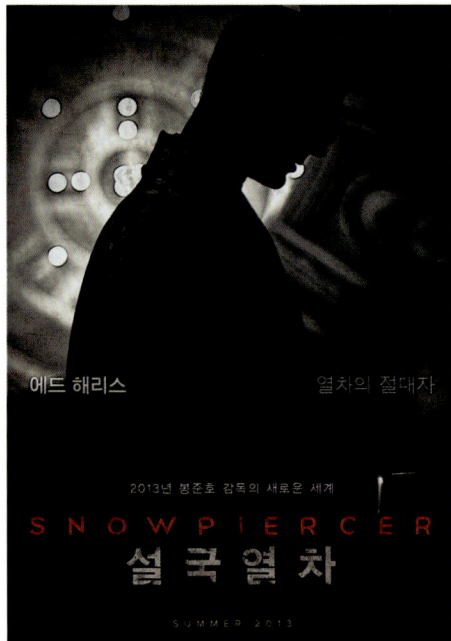

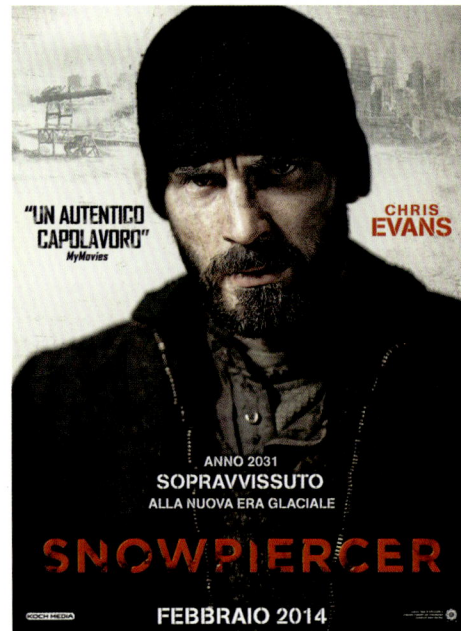

THIS SPREAD Various promotional images and marketing campaigns for the film.

From there it was a difficult road to getting the film released all around the world. It had been completed, in Director Bong's opinion, for some time and he was able to screen it for friends and at certain industry events. "It's quite ambiguous to talk about the first screening because with *The Host* and *Mother*, they all premiered at Cannes," he says. "But with *Snowpiercer*, because we went through the conflict with The Weinstein Company, the festival season sort of passed and the first time we showed the film with Tilda and all the actors was at the Deauville American Film Festival. They have the Deauville Asian Film Festival, but at the request of the distributors, we ended up showing it at the Deauville American Film Festival. I remember it was quite a different setup: the screen was quite small and far away from the audience. It stands out amongst the memories of all of my previous screenings. I do remember that we had the original writers of the graphic novel join us: Jean-Marc Rochette who drew the novel and Benjamin Legrand, who wrote parts two and three of the story. The writer of part one of the graphic novel—Jacques Lob—he actually passed away quite some time ago, but his widow came to our screening. This whole setup about humanity's survival, about the train, and the earth going through a new ice age, the whole setup and idea came from Jacques Lob, but we weren't able to talk with him, but his widow came and we talked about what kind of person Jacques was. She also brought a photo of him, so when we went up to the stage to introduce the film, she brought the photo up to the stage and showed it to the audience and that's something I remember in particular about the screening."

The movie as Director Bong envisioned it premiered in Seoul on the 29th July 2013, almost exactly a year after it had completed shooting. It then went on general release throughout Asia while the US cut was debated. Eventually, Bong Joon Ho won and his vision went out on limited release in June 2014 in North America. It has never received a cinema release in the UK, but in recent years, viewers there have been able to watch it on streaming services. *Snowpiercer* has been acclaimed and almost immediately hailed as a new classic in sci-fi cinema. It has been endlessly analyzed in articles and video essays, both in and of itself and also in regard to the rest of Director Bong's oeuvre.

"It was number one on iTunes for months and got a big following," remembers Durst. "Bong became a bit of a hero because he took on Weinstein and won. That was a pretty rare thing to happen. It was interesting: the whole process of it. The thing about Bong, he thinks ten years ahead. He just knows what's going to happen and goes for it with complete conviction."

CHAPTER EIGHT:

WE GO FORWARD

In the years since *Snowpiercer*'s release, the cult around the film—and around Director Bong—has only grown. The story as told in the graphic novels has continued, with a concluding fourth volume published in 2015, followed by a prequel series in 2019. The very last panel of *Le Transperceneige* shows a small area of dry land amidst the snow and a flower blooming on it.

2020 saw the premier of the *Snowpiercer* TV show. The show is unrelated to the movie or graphic novel but takes the core concept as its base. Focusing on the early days of the train, once the Earth has frozen, it features an ensemble confronting similar issues to the film and graphic novel that came before it: capitalism, justice, injustice, and personal freedom versus the common good. The show has brought new fans to *Snowpiercer*, fans who can now travel down the rabbit hole of the film that came before the series and the *bande dessinée* that preceded the film. Entirely not by design but by evolution, *Snowpiercer* has 'suddenly' become a franchise spanning forty years. As Chris Evans puts it, "It really is one of the films that I am most proud of. There's a timelessness to it and I do think it's gaining steam."

For Bong Joon Ho, he followed *Snowpiercer* four years later with *Okja*. The *Snowpiercer* train might have spanned Earth but *Okja* was a truly globe-trotting movie, from Seoul to New York and Vancouver for its story about a young girl out to save her best friend: a genetically engineered super pig. Reuniting him with various members of the Bong Joon Ho family—

Tilda Swinton, Dooho Choi, Catherine George—*Okja* played at the Cannes Film Festival and gained plaudits for its blend of character, adventure, inventiveness, and themes such as greed, injustice, fairness, and choice.

It was these topics that he would return to with razor-sharp focus and clarity of vision with 2019's *Parasite*. The story of the working-class Kim family who, posing as workers and family helpers, infiltrate the wealthy Park family, asks the question of who is dependent on whom? With its pitch-perfect acting, intricately designed direction and wholly original script, *Parasite* was a phenomenon. It is one of the most acclaimed South Korean films of all time, the highest grossing, and was the story of the 2020 Academy Awards®, winning: Best Picture, Best Director, Best International Feature Film, and Best Screenplay. But the film may not have come to pass at all if it were not for *Snowpiercer*.

RIGHT Timmy (Marcanthonee Reis) looks out at his new home: the outside world.
OPPOSITE Finished concept art showing Yona and Timmy in the aftermath of the explosion and derailment.

The two films share commonality—the rich/poor divide being the most obvious. But there is a unity of location, character, and story that makes both movies move like clockwork. The way in which the camera travels through each film, revealing geography and story in unison, that makes two movies that seem separated by genre united in execution.

It was during postproduction on *Snowpiercer* that the idea of *Parasite* first struck Director Bong and he, himself, has drawn comparisons between the two.

"I like what Bong says when he juxtaposes *Snowpiercer* to *Parasite*," remarks Eric Durst. "*Parasite* being a vertical film and *Snowpiercer* as a horizontal film. The societal structure: the shithole in the back with people in dregs and the king in the front who has this whole reasoning of why he needs to be who he is and all that kind of stuff, which is pretty contemporary now, particularly in America. I think it strikes a chord with a lot of people and I'm glad the film has been on streaming services, so people can see it now."

It is not unusual for concepts to occur to Bong Joon Ho while in the throes of another project. Tilda Swinton recalls how their collaborations have first been intimated, "Almost always just a single image or initiating gesture: With *Snowpiercer* it was the revolution from the rear to the front of the perpetual engine. With *Okja*, he just showed me one small drawing of a girl and a giant pig, holding it over the back of his car seat on our way to the airport in Seoul after the premiere of *Snowpiercer*. He sent me a similarly tantalizing drawing recently—the first green shoot of a new project, and with another, yet to be developed, a single sentence—a predicament. It's as if he drops a seed, a breadcrumb on the path. And that's all I ever need."

For many of the cast, crew, and friends on *Snowpiercer*, the years that have passed and the success of *Parasite* means more people discover *Snowpiercer* and the work of Bong Joon Ho than ever.

"When you come onto a project like this, you are taking a leap of faith," says Jamie Bell. "I say that only because I was ignorant, really. I didn't really know Bong's strength and his powers. I'd seen a couple of films, but I really think he kicked it into a different gear as well with his last two films. I think that *Parasite* is just a work of—we run out of superlatives to describe it. But when I saw *Snowpiercer* for the first time, I could see that it was something special... I think we've all seen the influence that this film's had and that can't be undermined. Bong knew what he was doing when he assembled his cast. A wholly unique and original film that really speaks to where the fuck we are as a society: we are on that train, basically, and it's going off the side of a cliff. So it was ahead of its time in so many ways, and I'm so honored and grateful to be a part of it. I can walk into a meeting and say 'I was in *Snowpiercer*. I was a part of that film.'"

The difficult questions the film asks have only become more relevant. The environmental concerns and the politics seem ever more like a mirror of this film, and for whatever may be the surface trappings of *Snowpiercer*, it is as personal and charged with feeling as any of Bong Joon Ho's works of art.

TILDA SWINTON'S FAVORITE MEMORY OF THE SHOOT WAS "JAMIE BELL WEARING MASON'S DETACHABLE BREASTS SO CASUALLY THAT BONG DID NOT NOTICE THEM FOR MOST OF ONE AFTERNOON."

LEFT The kronole bomb. Much like the train itself, it has been pieced together, bit by bit, toward its inevitable conclusion. Certain items, characters' possessions, have real and totemic weight in Bong Joon Ho's films, such as the golden pig in *Okja* and the scholar's rock in *Parasite*.
TOP A depiction of feeding time in the tail section.
ABOVE A concept artwork of Yona and Timmy leaving the train.
NEXT SPREAD Cast and crew gather in the train.

> ## "WHEN I THINK OF SNOWPIERCER, I IMMEDIATELY THINK OF PRAGUE. JUST BEING IN THAT BEAUTIFUL CITY WITH ACTORS AND CREW MEMBERS THAT I LOVE AND ADMIRE."
>
> BONG JOON HO

But wherever the world is and wherever the tracks are leading, the making of *Snowpiercer* is remembered fondly by all who worked on it.

Chris Evans: "It was an honor to be in such a committed environment with so many committed actors. Between Tilda Swinton and Octavia and Jamie and Ed Harris, there were just so many actors that... you can't buy any of them. Not to disparage other actors that take paychecks, because we do that from time to time, but it was a collection of actors who have incredible integrity and when they commit to something, they jump in with both feet. I just felt so honored to share the screen with them. Every day I came to set, I just felt so proud and pretty outclassed, if I'm honest."

Ewen Bremner: "There are many small moments that are fond memories. It was an uncommonly special time making that film. It was like we'd all taken some magic dust or something, and transported for a few hours."

Ed Harris: "I'd love to work with Bong again. He really is a master... He's gentle and such a sweet guy. I really did like him. He's a good man."

Eric Durst: "What struck me more than anything with Bong was just the fact that he's done his homework and has considered so much and he respects everybody so much. He's a beautiful guy to work with."

Julian Spencer: "That film was bloody brilliant to work on because all the people, all the heads of department, were chosen for their skill and it was great to see Director Bong just choose those people over a long period of time and get it all together. And we did it. The result speaks for itself, and it's a shame it didn't come out when we'd intended. A good job, I loved it; I wish I'd get more dream-team jobs like that."

Catherine George: "I found working with him incredible, I feel very lucky, now that the rest of the world has discovered Director Bong. He used to be our little secret!"

Jeremy Woodhead: "The release trauma of *Snowpiercer* is well documented, and it meant we never got a theatrical or streaming release in the UK. Now that it's finally available to view, it is so gratifying to get regular emails and texts from people who have finally got to see the film—and love it as much as I did being involved in it!"

Marco Beltrami: "I love how Bong's brain works. He's just so creative and thinks differently from so many other people. It was so refreshing. It was one of those projects that you don't get that often where you just enjoy every moment."

Ondej Nekvasil: "That kind of combination of a nice working experience plus the nice human experience—guys who are really in the same mode as you are, and have the same type of creativity in a way that you don't have to yell to everybody that you are an artist, because whatever you do is art. That kind of thing was very special for me. I'm not saying that because of this book, I'm saying it because it's true. That was very specific. That was really a very special time when we did that. You're working pretty hard, almost non-stop, but you feel that all you're doing makes sense."

Tilda Swinton: "It was a complete joy from start to finish."

Bong Joon Ho: "*Snowpiercer* was pretty much all shot in Prague, although the film doesn't include any shots of the city because it was all shot on set, so it has nothing to do with the actual film, but when I think of *Snowpiercer,* I immediately think of Prague. Just being in that beautiful city with actors and crew members that I love and admire, walking along the streets and enjoying conversations with them. I spent nine months in Prague in total, if you include preproduction and production, so it was a long period that I spent in the city. For me, *Snowpiercer* equals Prague."

As it says in the script, "Fade to white." And so, like the Snowpiercer's journey, we find ourselves back at the beginning.

ACKNOWLEDGMENTS

This book would not have been possible without the enthusiasm, help, and generosity of so many people. Titan Books and the author would like to thank: Bong Joon Ho, Dooho Choi, Ini Chung, Kevin Woo, Francis Chung, Jerry Ko, Yeonu Choi, Mina Hwang, Tilda Swinton, Chris Evans, Jamie Bell, Ewen Bremner, Octavia Spencer, Ed Harris, Eric Durst, Ondřej Nekvasil, Catherine George, Marco Beltrami, Julian Spencer, Jeremy Woodhead, Sharon Choi, Stephanie Hetherington, Laura Price, Amazing15, and Steven Ward.

FOR JOHN AND CLARK

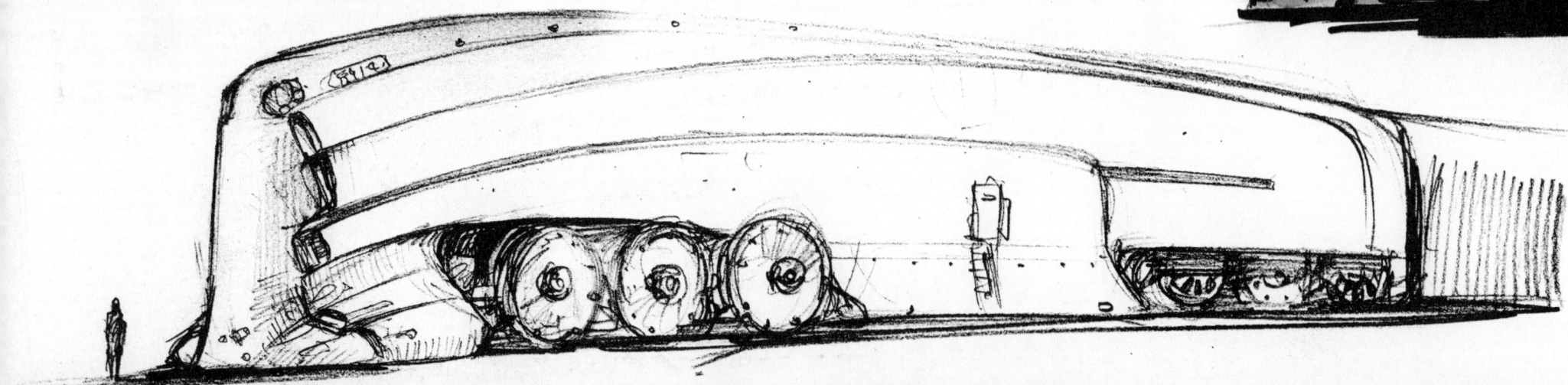